SCIENCE

Projects

& Activities

Content Development: Peter Rillero, Ph.D.

Publications International, Ltd.

Contributing Writers: Peter Rillero, Ph.D., Phyllis J. Perry, Ed.D., Karen E. Bledsoe, Candyce Norvell

Contributing Consultants: Nancy Goodman, Joseph Peters, Ph.D.

Contributing Illustrators: Terri and Joe Chicko, Steve Henry, John Jones, Ellen Joy Sasaki

Louis Weber, CEO
Publications International, Ltd.
7373 North Cicero Avenue
Lincolnwood, Illinois 60712

Permission is never granted for commercial purposes.

Manufactured in China.

8 7 6 5 4 3 2 1

ISBN: 0-7853-3775-X

Contents

Lively Science

WHAT IS science? You might think of science as a group of subjects that you study in school. Science *is* a collection of facts about the world. But another big part of science is experimentation. The hands-on science experiences in this book unite both aspects of science. The experiences will help you learn methods of doing science and discover facts about the world. And you will have fun!

This book covers many branches or subjects of science. The study of animals, plants, and other living organisms is called life sciences or biology. Chemistry studies substances; what they are made of, what characteristics they have, and how they react with each other. Physics deals with forces, motion, heat, and light. Astronomy is the study of stars, planets, and other spacey stuff. Earth sciences, such as geology (the study of rocks and the earth) and meteorology (the study of weather) look at the way the earth developed and how it constantly changes around us.

No matter which aspect of the world scientists study, they rely on their ability to make *observations*. They listen and look at the world around them to see what is there and how things act. Then, when they can, they take *measurements* as a way to describe their observations. Frequently, scientists try to *classify* (or organize) the information that they have gathered in a way that makes sense to them. Doing this makes it easier to understand the information. Scientists may take what they have learned and use it to form a *hypothesis* about what they are studying. A hypothesis is a guess, based on facts, of a possible answer to the *problem* they are trying to solve. To find out if the hypothesis is correct, scientists try to *test* it by doing more observation or by performing *experiments*. Whether or not a hypothesis is correct, scientists can still learn from the results.

Before you begin your own scientific explorations with the projects in this book, you should know a couple of things. Each project has one or more beakers by it. These show how difficult the project is. Easy projects get one test tube, medium projects get two, and challenging projects get three. If you'd like to do one of the challenging projects, but think it might be too hard, get help from a parent or from an older brother or sister.

Be careful as you do the projects in this book. Part of being a scientist is being responsible in what you do. Always think about how you can do a project safely. Never leave an experiment unattended unless you're sure that it is safe to do so. If you have younger brothers or sisters or pets, be sure that the project doesn't pose any danger to them. Also, make sure you always clean up after an experiment and dispose of materials properly. This is true whether you're working inside or outside.

Although only some of the projects require adult supervision, make sure that you always get permission to do a project. Show your parents the activity and get their approval before you start. Some projects contain a "Caution." These projects have potential dangers such as flames, sharp objects, or hazardous chemicals. You should only do these projects with help from an adult.

After you pick a project to do, read all of the instructions and check the "What You'll Need" list so that you know exactly what you'll need and what you'll have to do. Most of the projects in this book use items that you can find around your home. When you are planning the project, make sure you have enough time. Some projects can be done quickly. But others might have to sit for hours or days. You'll need to be sure to take care of the project during that time.

Some projects may turn out differently than you expected. That happens to all scientists. If it does happen to you, try to figure out why. Do the project again and see if that makes a difference. For projects that work as you expected, try to explain what happened. Observe what happens and think about it. That's the scientific way of learning.

The more projects and activities you do, the more science skills you will develop. And you'll be learning all about the world as you have fun with these crafts and activities. As your skill level grows and your knowledge increases, you will develop a love for science and new respect for the world in which we all live.

Chapter 1: # The Animal Kingdom

~~~~~~

THE BLUE JAY SWOOPS down out of the morning fog and grabs a wiggling earthworm from the grass. Meanwhile, a cat that has been watching the action suddenly stops and frantically scratches where a flea just nipped its skin. What do the blue jay, earthworm, cat, and flea have in common? They're all part of the animal kingdom.

When people think of animals they usually think of creatures with four legs and fur, like cats, dogs, cows, or deer. But these are all just one type of animal called mammals. Other groups of animals include: birds and reptiles; amphibians and fishes; starfishes; arthropods; mollusks and worms; and jellyfishes and sponges.

What exactly is an animal? From the huge killer whale to the small planaria (worm), animals come in many sizes and shapes. But, unlike bacteria, viruses, and algae, all animals are made up of many cells (or are "multicellular"). Also, animals don't make their own food like plants do. Animals must eat other living things to get their nutrients.

Get a little wild with the projects and activities in this chapter as you learn all about animals!

Gulping Fish

Count the gulps to see how water temperature affects breathing in fish.

What You'll Need:

two aquariums

four comet goldfish

two aquarium thermometers

paper and pen

FISH DON'T BREATHE the way you do. They get oxygen by gulping in water and pumping it over their gills. The gills are able to take oxygen from the water. In this activity you'll learn that water temperature affects a fish's ability to take in oxygen.

Set up two small fish tanks to hold two comet goldfish each. (Get advice from your local aquarium store on setting up the tanks.) Once the fish have settled into their new home, observe the temperature of the water by checking the tank thermometer.

It should be close to room temperature, between 65° and 70°F. Watch each of the four fish, and determine how many times per minute they gulp to take air from the water. Write these figures down.

Gradually add warm water to one tank, over a period of 20 minutes, to raise the temperature 5°F. Gradually add cool water to the other tank, over a period of 20 minutes, to lower the temperature 5°F. Do not change the temperature too fast, as this can be harmful to the fish. Record the gulping rates of all four fish again.

What were your results? Did the fish gulp faster in warm water than in cool water? Warm water contains less oxygen than cool water, so fish in warm water have to work harder to get the oxygen they need from the water.

On the Right Track

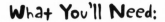

Try to identify animal tracks and take a sample to study.

What You'll Need:

old toothbrush

empty milk carton

scissors

paper clips

water

measuring cup

plaster of Paris

wooden stick

ANIMALS OF THE SAME SPECIES show differences in their tracks. Go to a nearby park or other public place where people frequently walk their dogs. Find tracks left by dogs, and examine them closely. Count how many different sets of tracks you can make out. Select one footprint, and use an old toothbrush to brush away any debris in the track. Cut a strip about 1½ inches wide and 8 inches long from a milk carton; leave the bottom of the carton intact. Bend the strip into a circle, and hold the ends together with a couple of paper clips. Put your circle around the footprint.

Put 1 cup of water in the bottom half of your milk carton. Stir in 1 cup of plaster of Paris. Fill the collar around the animal's track to the top with the plaster, and smooth it with a stick. Bend a paper clip to make a hanger, and poke one end into the plaster. Let everything sit for 30 minutes. Be very careful when working with the plaster; it can be difficult to clean up. When the plaster is dry to the touch, peel away the cardboard. Lift up your mold of the track. After two hours, you can rinse the plaster in running water. When it is dry, you can hang up the track by the paper clip hanger.

Pulse

This project really has a lot of heart.

What You'll Need:

paper and pen

watch with a second hand

YOU MAY KNOW that your pulse rate varies. After you exercise, for example, your heart beats faster. Pulse rates also vary from one individual to another. Do you think that younger or older people might have faster heart rates? Do you think that males or females will have faster heart rates? Is a person's pulse rate higher in the morning or evening? Write your answers down.

Draw five columns on a sheet of paper, and label them "NAME," "AGE," "SEX," "TIME," and "RATE." Ask friends and family members if you can test them. Put your first two fingers on the underside of the subject's wrist below their thumb. Count how many pulse beats you feel in 30 seconds, and multiply that number by 2. Record this on your chart, and fill in all the other information. Try to check each subject four times, twice in the morning and twice in the evening. Does the information you gathered agree with your guesses?

Healthy Pressure

When your heart beats, the arteries expand and contract. This is why you feel a pulse. The average pulse rate for adults is 72 beats per minute.

Gotcha!

Have you seen movies in which someone digs a pit as a trap for a lion or tiger? You can make the same kind of trap—for much smaller game.

What You'll Need:

glass jar

hand trowel or shovel

four flat rocks

small board

MAKE YOUR SAFE INSECT TRAP in a place where there's likely to be a lot of bug traffic. Under a bush is good. First get a glass jar. Dig a hole that is the same size as the jar so you can set the jar down in the hole. The top of the jar should be almost even with the ground.

Now put four small, flat rocks around the top of the jar, and set a board on the rocks. The board will keep rain and bug-eating animals out of the jar. The rocks will allow enough room for bugs to fall into the trap. Leave your trap overnight. In the morning, see what you've caught. Can you identify what's in the jar? After you've studied your bug collection, be sure to let those bugs go and fill up the hole you dug.

Beetle Mania!

When is a worm not a worm? When it's really a beetle!
Observe the growth of these amazing insects.

What You'll Need:

mealworms

glass jar with lid

bran or oatmeal

apple or potato

water

SOME CREATURES GO THROUGH BIG CHANGES during their lives. One example is the mealworm, also known as the mealy worm. You can buy these at a pet store and watch them "grow up" into adult beetles. Put your mealworms in a glass jar with some raw bran or oatmeal. Also put in some pieces of raw apple or potato for the meal-worms to eat. Sprinkle a little water in the jar and put on the lid. (Make some small holes in the lid so air can get in.) The mealworms will morph into flour beetles. There are more than 300,000 types of beetles in the world. Some of the largest—the Goliath beetles—can grow as big as your fist!

Take Cover

At first glance, it may look like beetles have two sets of wings. However, the front "wings" are actually sheaths (or covers) for the real wings in back. These sheaths protect the beetle's wings when it is not flying. The scientific name for beetles is Coleoptera, which means "sheath-winged."

Preserve a Spiderweb

The spider is truly one of nature's great artists.
See how you can preserve one of their masterpieces.

What You'll Need:

empty spiderweb

talcum powder

black construction
paper

hair spray

To do this project, you'll need to find a spiderweb that isn't occupied. To find out if there's a spider in the web, tap it very lightly. If a spider is in the web, it will move and you'll see it. If the web is someone's home, find another web to preserve.

When you find an empty web, sprinkle talcum powder all over it to make it easier to see. Then, ask an adult to help you apply hair spray to a piece of black construction paper. While the spray is still wet, bring the paper up against into the web so that the web sticks to the paper. You've just preserved one of nature's great works of art!

Wiggly Workers

Earthworms have been called "a gardener's best friend." Find out why.

What You'll Need:

wide-mouth glass jar

garden soil

peat

sand

water

earthworms

dead leaves

paper bag

To make a wormery, first get a large jar that has a wide opening. Put in a layer of soil, a layer of peat, and a layer of sand. Water the soil well. Now dig some worms from a garden and put them in your wormery. Don't bury the worms! They'll take care of that themselves. But do cover the worms with some dead leaves. Set a paper bag over the top of the jar. This will keep out light, but let in the oxygen that worms need. Now put the jar in a cool place out of direct sunlight.

Keep your wormery damp and keep an eye on the earthworms. Can you guess why gardeners like earthworms? It's because they digest and pass soil through their bodies, loosening the soil and mixing nutrients. Plants grow better in looser soil with plenty of oxygen. Once you've seen the worms work, put them back where you got them.

Little Wigglers

Have you noticed the bright pink ring on earthworms? This contains their eggs, which will be left in the soil to hatch into new earthworms.

Making Tracks

You may not think that snails can do much.
But with a little help from you, they can be artists!

What You'll Need:

garden snails

black construction paper

talcum powder

HAVE A SNAIL HUNT and see if you can collect several snails. (Be gentle! Those shells may be fragile!) Snails are nocturnal, which means they like to sleep during the day and come out at night. You can usually find them sleeping in damp dark places, such as under a rock. One way to catch snails is to put a large clay flower pot upside down, with one side propped up, overnight in a garden.

Once you've found some snails, put them on a sheet of black construction paper and let them do what they do—crawl around. You'll be able to see the slimy trail they leave. When the paper is criss-crossed with snail tracks, carefully put the snails back where you found them.

Sprinkle talcum powder on their tracks. Tap off the excess talcum powder, and admire your snail art.

Polar Bear Warmth

〰〰〰〰〰〰〰〰〰〰〰〰〰〰〰〰〰〰

How do polar bears stay warm in the freezing cold of the Arctic? Use coffee to find the answer.

What You'll Need:

coffee

two glass jars

cloth

plastic wrap

food thermometer

POUR ONE CUP of strong black coffee (that has cooled to room temperature) into each of two clear glass jars. Cover one jar with a piece of white cloth, and the other jar with a piece of clear plastic wrap. Then put both jars in the sun for an hour or more. Use a food thermometer to check the temperature of the coffee in each jar. Which is warmer? Can you explain why?

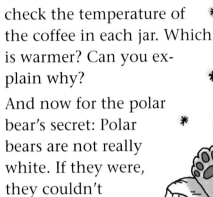

And now for the polar bear's secret: Polar bears are not really white. If they were, they couldn't stay warm in their Arctic habitat. As you just learned, white reflects sunlight and the heat that comes with it. The hairs in a polar bear's coat are clear. The hollow center of each hair soaks up light from the sun, and the light filters out the sides. That's what makes polar bears look white. Each clear hair carries heat from the sun down to the polar bear's skin. Its skin is black, which means it soaks up heat to keep the bear warm. A polar bear is like the plastic-covered coffee in your experiment: Clear on the outside, black on the inside—and plenty warm!

What Hairy Feet You Have!

While you probably knew that polar bears live in cold climates, did you know that their feet have hair on the bottom of them? Well, they do—that's what keeps the bears from slipping on the ice.

Frog Raft

Ahoy! Who wants to go for a sail on a miniature raft just for frogs?

What You'll Need:

board (18 inches long, one inch thick)

candle or small lantern

2-inch-long nail (if using candle)

plastic bag (if using lantern)

heavy twine

large screw eye

 IF YOU HAVE ACCESS TO A POND you can visit at night, go frog "hunting." Shine a flashlight out over the pond and watch for glittering frog eyes. Then launch a frog raft and see if you can get any passengers.

With help from an adult, insert a screw eye in one end of your board and tie the end of your twine to it. For a light, drive a nail all the way through the board. Stick a candle on the pointed end that comes through the board. If your nights are too breezy for candle flames, omit the nail

and candle, and use a small battery-powered lantern instead. It won't be as attractive as a flickering candle flame, but it may still attract frogs. Seal the lantern in a heavy plastic bag, then have an adult help you tie it to the board. Put the raft in the water and give it a push, then wait quietly for frogs to jump aboard. See how many passengers your raft will attract.

An Orange Frog?
Yes, it's true. While most frogs you see are green or brown, they come in all types of colors, including red, orange, blue, and black. It's also possible for the common green frog to look orange if that frog has too much yellow pigment in his skin.

Going Batty

Ever heard the expression "blind as a bat"? Bats do have poor vision, but they have a special way of "seeing." Find out how by playing bat tag.

What You'll Need:

blindfold

BATS GET AROUND BY USING "echolocation." (Break it into two smaller words, "echo" and "location.") Bats fly around squeaking all the time. Their squeaks "bounce" off objects and echo back to the bat's big ears. Bats use the echo to tell the location of the object. This works so well that they can zero in on (and eat) hundreds of mosquitoes and other bugs in a single night.

To play bat tag, you'll need a group of people. You'll also need a big, open area with no trees or other things to run into! Choose someone to be the "bat." The others will be insects. Blindfold the bat. The other players spread out. Once the game begins, the bat begins to squeak. The player that is facing the bat should squeak back, like an echo. The bat can move around, but the other players do not move. The bat has to find and tag the other players by listening to their squeaks. When each "insect" is tagged, it stops squeaking. The last "insect" to be tagged is the bat next time.

Clean As a . . . Bat?

Bats have a terrible reputation, and lots of people think they're unclean. But bats wash themselves like cats do, licking their fur very carefully. They comb themselves with their claws, too, and they clean out their ears with a knuckle. Bats are actually very clean mammals.

Understanding Your Pet

If you have a dog, cat, or another pet, listen to it and watch it to see how it communicates with you and other animals.

What You'll Need:

notebook

pen

markers

Watch your pet's eyes, ears, tail, paws, and fur. And watch their whole bodies. Try to figure out what they "say" by using their bodies. Does your dog or cat ever run back and forth between you and her food bowl? Or between you and the door? ("Lemme outta here!") Does your pet roll over and look at you to let you know she wants a tummy rub?

Animals also use their voices in more ways than you might think. How many different barks does your dog have, and what do they all mean? He probably has one bark for "Someone's at the door!" and another bark for "Hey, you stepped on my paw!" He probably also growls, whines, and makes other sounds. Each sound means he's trying to communicate with you or another animal. It's the same with cats. They may have one meow to say, "Feed me!" and another to say, "Can I come in now?"

Try making a pet dictionary where you record all the different ways your pets communicate, and what you think each thing means. You could draw pictures of what your pets look like when they're "saying" different things. The more you pay attention to your pets, the better you'll understand them.

Look at That Beak!

*And those feet, too! Learn how birds use their beak
and feet to help them survive in the wild.*

What You'll Need:

field guide to birds

poster board

markers

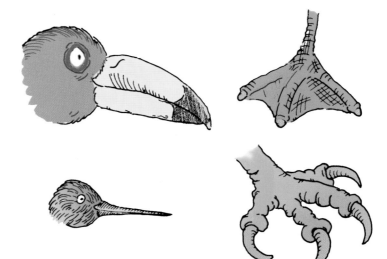

ONE OF THE EASIEST WAYS to identify different birds is by looking at their beaks. Some have sharp beaks for pecking. Others have long, wide, flat, or curved beaks. How does each bird's beak help it get food? (A pelican's beak, for example, expands to hold the fish it catches.)

Now think about birds' feet. Some have powerful feet with claws called "talons." Other feet, like a duck's webbed feet, are designed to help birds swim. How does a bird's feet help it move around in its habitat?

Look through a field guide to birds and pay special attention to birds' beaks and feet. Then make a chart showing the beaks and feet of different birds and telling how they help the birds survive.

What a Beak!

The South American swordbill is a bird whose bill is as long as its head and body put together! This bird lives in the South American rain forest, and she needs her long beak to gather her food, the nectar from the long, tube-shaped flowers of the passiflora plant. The bird's bill can be as long as four full inches.

Favorite Foods

Different kinds of birds have very different ideas about what makes a nice meal. See which birds eat which foods.

What You'll Need:

pie plates

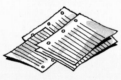

several kinds of bird food (birdseed, sunflower seeds, oats, bread crumbs)

paper

pen

FIRST, GATHER SEVERAL DIFFERENT KINDS of bird food, including birdseed, sunflower seeds, oats, bread crumbs, and anything else you can think of. Put each kind of food in a separate pie plate, then put all the pie plates outside, a few feet apart. Watch from a distance or from inside to see which kinds of birds eat which foods. Keep a record of this.

Try putting some of the pie plates on the ground, and some up high in bird feeders or trees, and watch what happens. Then, switch the pie plates around. Put the ones that were on the ground up high. What do you discover? You'll probably see that some birds prefer to eat on the ground, while others only eat in the trees. Birds may ignore even their favorite food if it's in the wrong place! If you try this activity at different times of the year, you may see different kinds of birds.

Beak Breakers

The beak of a bird influences the type of food it can eat. For example, big, strong beaks are used for breaking open seeds and nuts.

Examine a Bird Feather

Take a closer look at the complex structure of feathers. You could start a bird notebook to add to whenever you study your fine, feathered friends!

What You'll Need:

feathers

gloves

magnifying glass

notebook

NEXT TIME YOU FIND BIRD FEATHERS outdoors, take some time for a closer look. (Some bird feathers carry disease, so be careful to wear gloves when you handle them.) If you keep a bird notebook, you can add this information to your notes. Most feathers you find will have a hollow quill running down the center. Coming out of both sides of the quill are barbs. Look at them carefully with your magnifying glass. Notice the small, hooklike barbules that make the barbs stick together.

Feathers come in three basic types: Down feathers have no quill to speak of. The barbs are soft, and the barbules do not stick together. Body (or contour) feathers have downy barbs at the base for insulation, while the upper part forms a flat, windproof layer. Flight feathers do not have any downy parts at all. They are long and stiff, and they form the shape of the wings.

Draw your findings in your notebook. Using the color and the size of the feather, see if you can figure out what bird it came from. When you are done looking at the feather, put it back where you found it. Laws that protect our nation's birds also protect bird parts. Some feathers can be collected by permit only.

Chapter 2

The Plant Kingdom

WHAT DO a blade of grass and an oak tree have in common? Well, they both make the world more beautiful and have green leaves that produce nutrients and give off oxygen. And, in short, they are both plants.

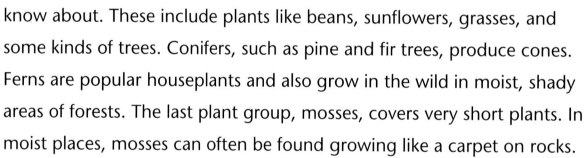

There are many types of plants in the plant kingdom, including: flowering plants, conifers, ferns, and mosses. Flowering plants make up most of the plants you know about. These include plants like beans, sunflowers, grasses, and some kinds of trees. Conifers, such as pine and fir trees, produce cones. Ferns are popular houseplants and also grow in the wild in moist, shady areas of forests. The last plant group, mosses, covers very short plants. In moist places, mosses can often be found growing like a carpet on rocks.

Plants produce the food for the animal kingdom. Animals get their nutrition by eating plants or by eating animals that eat plants. Animals also need oxygen. In a process called photosynthesis, plants use sunlight, carbon dioxide, and water in order to make their food. Luckily for animals, oxygen is given off in the process.

While working on the projects in this chapter, use only sterile (store-bought) potting soil. This will prevent fungal diseases such as "damping off." Have some fun, and, chances are, you will do some growing of your own!

Plants From Leaves

Not every plant needs to be grown from seed.
Sometimes the key is in the leaf!

What You'll Need:

African violet plant

scissors

clear plastic cup

water

paper and pen

four flowerpots and saucers

string

small rocks

potting soil

vermiculite

USING SCISSORS, snip off four healthy leaves from an African violet plant. Set these leaves in a clear plastic cup of water in a sunny window. Write down the date when you began this activity. Check on the leaves once a day. If you notice any change, write down your observations and the date. Eventually small leaves and new roots will begin to grow from the leaves.

Prepare four flowerpots for your sprouting leaves. Put a string in the pot so that the top of the string is near the top of the pot and a few inches of the string dangles out of the bottom hole. Put an inch of small rocks for drainage in the bottom of each pot. Fill the pots with a mixture of potting soil and vermiculite. Plant each of the sprouting leaves in its own pot. Put each pot on a saucer. Pour water into each saucer. The string will allow water from the saucer to travel up into the pot to keep the soil moist. Water as needed, and watch as a whole plant grows from each of the leaves you picked.

Budding Branches

In nature, plants have all kinds of ways to reproduce. Some trees, such as willows and poplars, can propagate new trees through fallen branches. Under the right conditions, a new tree will develop roots and grow out of the fallen branch.

Beans in the Dark

Cast some light on learning about plant growth.

What You'll Need:

lima beans

glass

water

two plastic foam cups

small rocks

sand

potting soil

SOAK SIX LIMA BEANS OVERNIGHT in a glass of water. Take two plastic foam cups, and put about 1 inch of small rocks in the bottom of each one. Add 1 inch of sand to each cup on top of the rocks, and then add about 4 inches of potting soil to each cup.

Plant the six bean seeds, three in each cup. Water each cup to keep the soil moist but not wet. Put one cup in a sunny windowsill and the other in a dark closet. Check on your beans every day to see how they're growing. Are you surprised by the results?

After several days, the plants growing on your windowsill will probably be healthy and green. The plants in the closet will be very pale, but they might be taller than the other plants. Plant cells have special light receptors. When they don't get enough light, they signal the plant to grow long and thin to seek out a light source. Because there's limited light, the plants in the closet don't produce the chlorophyll that makes the plants green and also absorbs sunlight to produce food. If you move the pale plants to the window, they will soon become green as well.

Mexican Jumping Beans

Frogs and rabbits can jump, but have you ever heard of a jumping bean? This type of Mexican bean seed has a small caterpillar living inside of it. When the caterpillar moves, the bean has to move, too. This jumping can last for several months until the caterpillar finally emerges from the bean as a small moth!

See Cells

Take a closer look at plants than you ever have before.

What You'll Need:

microscope with about 50-power magnification
(if you do not have your own microscope, you may be able to borrow one from your school)

a plant with thin leaves or an onion skin

glass slides

water

eyedropper

SET UP YOUR MICROSCOPE on a table. Find a plant with thin leaves, such as a common fern—or use a piece of onion skin. Place a leaf on a glass slide. Add one drop of water, and place a cover slide over the leaf and water. Look at the slide under your microscope. You should be able to make out box-shaped structures. These are plant cells. If you look closely, you should be able to see tiny green parts in the cells. These contain chlorophyll, which gives the plant its color and helps the plant produce food.

Plant Cell Particulars

Plant cells contain a cell wall that animal cells don't have. Plant cells also have one large vacuole (a fancy word for a small space), which is filled with water and nutrients. Leaf cells have green chloroplasts for photosynthesis. These are essential in a plant's production of nutrients.

Nut-rageous!

Crack some nuts and learn more about what's inside.

What You'll Need:

shelled nuts (cashew, walnut, pecan)

needle

cork

metal cup

water

thermometer

matches

tongs

pen and paper

FIND DIFFERENT KINDS OF NUTS that are about the same size. Stick one of the nuts on a needle, and stick the other end of the needle in a cork so it will stand by itself on a table. Put about ¼ inch of water in a metal cup. Measure the starting temperature of the water in the cup with a thermometer. Have an adult light the nut with a match. Using tongs, hold the cup over the flame. When the nut stops burning, record the temperature of the water. Compare that to the starting temperature to see how much the water's temperature increased. Repeat this experiment with a different kind of nut. Which has the most energy?

Nuts contain a great deal of food energy in the form of oils. When we eat nuts, our bodies take this energy and either use it or store it as fat. When you burned the nuts, their food energy was released as light and heat, which raised the temperature of the water.

Caution: *This project requires adult supervision.*

Make a Plant Press

A plant press is easy to make and even easier to use.

What You'll Need:

**two thin boards
(about 8″×10″)**

saw

**corrugated
cardboard**

newspaper

scissors

paper towels

**nylon webbing straps
(one-inch wide)**

four D-rings

plants

HAVE AN ADULT HELP YOU cut two thin boards to about the size of a paper towel. Then cut sheets of sturdy cardboard the same size as your boards. Cut newspaper sheets twice the size of your paper towels and fold them in half.

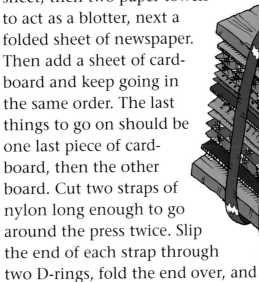

Lay down one board, then a cardboard sheet, then two paper towels to act as a blotter, next a folded sheet of newspaper. Then add a sheet of cardboard and keep going in the same order. The last things to go on should be one last piece of cardboard, then the other board. Cut two straps of nylon long enough to go around the press twice. Slip the end of each strap through two D-rings, fold the end over, and sew in place. Ask an adult to melt the other end in a flame to prevent fraying. Then wrap each strap once around the press and slip the free end through both D-rings. Turn the strap back, slip it through the bottom D-ring, and pull the strap to tighten. (If you have trouble figuring out how to complete this step, take a look at how your backpack straps work.)

To press plants: Lay them inside the folded newspapers and spread them out so they don't overlap. Arrange leaves and petals so that they lay flat. Build up your press as described above, using as many cardboard sheets and paper towel blotters as you need. Squeeze the layers together, strap the press tightly, and put it in a warm place for a week or more to dry.

Cycle of Life

A small plant can demonstrate nature's ability to recycle.

What You'll Need:

plant

large jar with lid

WATER A SMALL POTTED PLANT WELL. Then put the plant—pot and all—in a big, wide-mouthed jar and put the lid on tightly. Put the jar where it will get sunlight, and leave it there for 30 days. (Be careful that it doesn't get too hot or you could hurt the plant.) Observe what happens in the jar. Droplets of water will collect on the jar and drip down into the soil so the plant can use the water again. Because this is a self-contained system, the plant can live "on its own" inside the sealed jar (for a little while—eventually the plant would need fresh air; new, nutrient-rich soil; and if the plant grew large enough, a bigger pot).

Water, Water Everywhere!

In the water cycle, water evaporates from lakes and oceans. Then it condenses into clouds. Eventually it falls back to the earth as precipitation, which could be rain, snow, or sleet.

Root View Box

*Plants grow two ways—up out of the soil and down into the ground.
Use this special box to watch how roots grow.*

What You'll Need:

**half-gallon
milk carton**

scissors

sheet of glass

**clear acrylic or stiff
clear plastic
packaging**

craft glue or tape

potting soil

**seeds of vegetables
with large roots**

pan or tray

cardboard

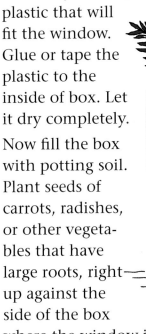

CUT OFF THE TOP OF THE MILK CARTON and punch a few holes in the bottom for drainage. Cut a window in the side, leaving a ½-inch margin all the way around the window. Have an adult cut a sheet of glass or clear acrylic to fit the window inside the box. Another option is to check all the plastic packaging that is to be recycled in your house for a piece of stiff, clear plastic that will fit the window. Glue or tape the plastic to the inside of box. Let it dry completely.

Now fill the box with potting soil. Plant seeds of carrots, radishes, or other vegetables that have large roots, right up against the side of the box where the window is. Set the carton on a pan or tray to

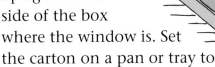

catch extra water, then water the seeds well. Put a bit of cardboard under the bottom of the box on the side opposite the window. This will tilt the box slightly, so the roots will grow right up against the window. Check the plants' growth to see how the roots are developing. Be sure to give your plants enough water and light. If you want to do this as a science-fair project, be sure to plant the seeds at least eight weeks ahead of time.

I See the Light

No matter what, plants always grow toward light!

What You'll Need:

plastic cup

potting soil

pinto beans

scissors

cardboard

shoe box

FIRST, PUNCH A FEW drainage holes in the bottom of a cup, add some potting soil, then plant a few pinto beans. Water the beans and put them in a warm place. Next, tape two pieces of cardboard into a shoe box to make a maze, as shown. Cut a hole in one end of the shoe box. Be sure to keep the soil moist. When the beans sprout, put the cup in the shoe box. Put the lid on the shoe box.

Take the lid off the box every day to look at the bean plants and to water them as needed (keep the soil moist, but not dripping wet). Always be sure to put the lid back. Which way are the plants growing? See how long it takes them to grow out of the hole and into the light.

Go Into the Light

Plants grow toward light. This action is called phototropism. Plants have hormones called auxins, which cause the phototropism.

Vegetable in a Bottle

This trick will mystify everyone—but it takes a lot of patience!

What You'll Need:

clear plastic bottle with a narrow mouth (such as a soft drink bottle)

garden vegetable plant (such as cucumber or zucchini)

wooden box (optional)

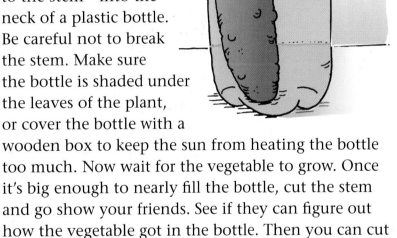

FIND SOMEONE friendly who has a vegetable garden and who is willing to help you. Watch for a garden plant to blossom and produce fruit. Cucumbers, zucchini, or gourds will work well for this project. Slip the tiny vegetable—still attached to the stem—into the neck of a plastic bottle. Be careful not to break the stem. Make sure the bottle is shaded under the leaves of the plant, or cover the bottle with a wooden box to keep the sun from heating the bottle too much. Now wait for the vegetable to grow. Once it's big enough to nearly fill the bottle, cut the stem and go show your friends. See if they can figure out how the vegetable got in the bottle. Then you can cut away the bottle to get the vegetable out.

Fruits in Vegetable Clothing

Cucumbers and zucchini are often called vegetables, but a botanist would call them fruits (a botanist studies plants). Fruits are the ripened parts of plants that contain seeds.

Seed Collections

You'll be surprised by how interesting and attractive seeds can be!

What You'll Need:

seeds

small bottles or clear film canisters

masking tape

flower guide

pen

strip of thin wood

sandpaper

varnish

craft glue

BEGIN COLLECTING SEEDS around your house. Look for garden flowers, grasses, and weeds that have gone to seed. Gather seeds from fruits and vegetables in the kitchen. Use small bottles or clear film canisters to store the seeds. (You can get film canisters from a photo developer.) Use masking tape to label the bottles. A flower guide can help you identify the plants. When collecting seeds from wild plants, be sure to get permission from the property owner. Never collect plants or plant parts from state or national forests.

When you have 10 or 20 different kinds of seeds collected, you can use tiny glass bottles to display them. (Always be careful when handling glass.) Ask an adult to help you sand and varnish a 1-inch-wide strip of wood. Glue the bottles in a row on the wood strip. Put a different kind of seed in each bottle and screw the caps on tightly. Glue a label under each sample to identify it.

Natural Savings Account

People concerned about the extinction of plants are creating seed banks. If a plant goes extinct in the wild, the seeds can then be used to reintroduce the plants.

Mini-Greenhouses

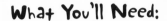

Winter is the perfect time to start seeds indoors for a spring garden.

What You'll Need:

**small containers
or soup cans**

potting soil

water

**flower or
vegetable seeds**

plastic bags

 PUNCH SOME HOLES in the bottom of your containers for drainage. Fill them with soil. Wet the soil and set the containers aside to drain.

Plant only two or three seeds in each container. As a rule, plant the seed no deeper than four times its diameter. (Some seeds need to be planted on top of the soil because they need light to sprout—check the directions on the package.) Put each container in a plastic bag, like the kind that grocery stores use for fruits and vegetables. Gather up the mouth of the bag and blow into it, then tie off the top with a twist-tie to make a miniature greenhouse.

Set the greenhouse in a warm room. Once you see sprouts, put your greenhouses in a sunny window. It's also a good idea to take the greenhouses outdoors on warm days where they can get more sun for a few hours each day.

The first green "leaves" on your seedlings are called "seed leaves." They are not real leaves, but parts of the seed. Wait until the seedlings have at least four actual leaves and are tall and strong before transplanting them outdoors.

Do Plants Breathe?

Even though plants don't breathe like you do, they still need air.

What You'll Need:

plant

petroleum jelly

TOO SEE HOW PLANTS TAKE AIR IN AND OUT, get a small plant with lots of leaves. Cover the tops of five leaves with a heavy coat of petroleum jelly. Then cover the undersides of five other leaves with a heavy coat of petroleum jelly.

Look at the plants each day for a week. What happens? What does this tell you about how plants take air in and out? There are openings on the undersides of leaves. Air moves in and out of those openings, allowing a plant to "breathe."

Plant Your Socks?

Imagine what would happen if your socks started to sprout.

What You'll Need:

pair of old, worn-out tube socks

shallow aluminum foil pan

water

GET A PAIR OF OLD TUBE SOCKS and put them on over your shoes. Go for a walk through a field of tall grass and weeds. (The best time to do this is in the early fall, but you can try it in spring and summer, too.) Carefully take off the socks once they are covered with seeds. When you get home, put the socks in a shallow aluminum foil pan with a little water in the bottom. There should be just enough water to make the socks wet—no more. Put the pan in a place indoors where it will get plenty of light, and keep those socks moist. In a few days, the seeds that stuck to your socks will begin to sprout. Let your sock garden grow for a while to see what kinds of plants you have.

Natural Dyes

Before there were chemical dyes, people had to make their own dyes from plant materials. Try your hand at dyeing a shirt or bandanna.

What You'll Need:

wool or cotton material to dye

laundry detergent

knife

glass bowl

water

stainless steel pan

sieve

alum (available in the spice rack at grocery stores)

a variety of colorful plant material (see chart at right)

YOU'LL NEED AN ADULT TO HELP YOU with the cutting and boiling in this project.

1. Wash cotton or wool material in detergent—do not use fabric softener.

2. Cut up your plant material. Chop up or crush hard materials such as roots. Soak it

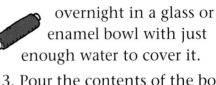

overnight in a glass or enamel bowl with just enough water to cover it.

3. Pour the contents of the bowl into a stainless steel pan. Bring to a boil on the stove and simmer gently for about one hour. Check the pan frequently and add water when needed.

Here are some of the colors you can make from common plants.

Plant	Color
Onion skins	yellow
Goldenrod flowers	yellow
Carrots	yellow
Red onions	pink
Raspberries	pink
Beets	rose
Coffee	brown
Nut hulls (not shells)	brown
Grass	green
Spinach	green

4. Strain the dye through a sieve back into the bowl to remove plant material. Allow the liquid to cool.

5. Measure the liquid. For every quart of dye, add one half ounce of alum (about one tablespoon). Alum is a mordant. That means it helps set the dye.

6. Wet your fabric and wring it out, then put it in the steel pan with your dye. Put the pan on the stove and simmer slowly until the fabric is just a little darker than you want it. (The fabric will look lighter when it dries.) Remember that natural colors will be soft, not bright.

7. Move the pan to the sink and pour everything through a strainer. Run a little cold water over your fabric to cool and rinse it. Wring it out and hang it up to dry outdoors where the drips won't hurt anything.

A Tomato-Berry?

Berries are an important food, but they are also far more widespread than is commonly thought. Plants that produce berries include grapes, blueberries, currants, tomatoes, bananas, eggplants, and dates. There are other foods that are closely related to the berry family, as well. Pumpkins, squashes, and cucumbers are pepos, which are a special kind of berry. Oranges, lemons, and grapefruit are another type of berry.

Shout About Sprouts

It's easy and fun to grow tasty sprouts for salads and sandwiches.

What You'll Need:

alfalfa seeds

quart jar

cheesecloth

rubber band

teaspoon

WASH AND DRY THE JAR. Measure two teaspoons of alfalfa seeds into the jar. Fill the jar half-full with water. Cover the top with three layers of cheesecloth, holding the cheesecloth in place with a rubber band. Swirl the jar around to rinse the seeds, and pour the water out through the cheesecloth.

Place the jar in a warm, dry place, such as a cupboard. The seeds should begin to sprout in a day or two. Each day, take the jar out, add more water, swirl to rinse the seeds, and pour the water out through the cheesecloth. When the sprouts are about two inches long, place the jar in a sunny window for a few days to green up. Keep rinsing the sprouts every day. After the sprouts have greened, put them in the refrigerator.

Seed Specifics

Seeds need moisture, oxygen, and the right temperature to sprout or germinate. Most seeds don't need light to germinate.

Venus Flytraps

*Carnivorous plants can be easy and fun to raise
if you give them the right environment.*

What You'll Need:

**small aquarium,
fish bowl, or
1-gallon glass jar**

**charcoal, potting
soil, sand, and peat
moss (use materials
especially prepared
for use with plants)**

old mixing bowl

water

Venus flytrap plant

**insects or tiny bits
of raw meat**

POUR A ONE-INCH LAYER of crushed charcoal into the bottom of the terrarium. Mix three parts of potting soil with one part sand and one part peat moss in an old mixing bowl. Add water until the mix is moist but not soggy. Put about three inches of the mix into the terrarium. Now dig a small hole for your plant. Carefully remove the Venus flytrap from its pot and plant it in the hole. Put a cover on the terrarium. You need to keep your plant moist. Most purchased Venus flytrap plants die because of improper care. Venus flytraps are bog plants, so they need humid air and wet soil to survive.

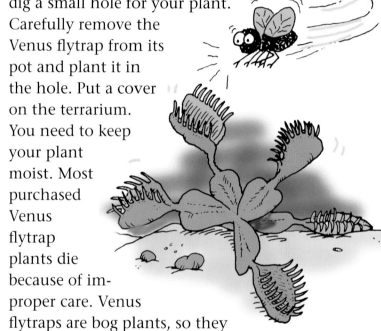

The Venus flytrap eats insects in order to get nutrients—since bog soils are low in nutrients. You can feed your plant small insects or tiny bits of raw meat. Put a bit of meat on a leaf and gently tap it to make the leaf close. Be aware that Venus flytraps are becoming rare because of over-collection. Many are collected illegally. When you buy yours, check the label to see if it has been raised in a greenhouse or collected from the wild. Be sure to only purchase greenhouse-raised plants.

Surviving in the Desert

Have you ever wondered how desert plants live on very little water?

What You'll Need:

paper towels

water

cookie sheet

paper clips

waxed paper

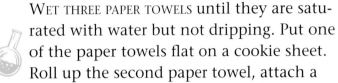

WET THREE PAPER TOWELS until they are saturated with water but not dripping. Put one of the paper towels flat on a cookie sheet. Roll up the second paper towel, attach a paper clip to it to keep it rolled up, and put it on the cookie sheet, too. Put the third paper towel on a piece of waxed paper that is the same size. Roll up the waxed paper and the paper towel together, and attach a paper clip to them so they stay rolled up.

Leave all three paper towels where they are for 24 hours. Then check them. The flat one will be dry. The rolled one will be dry or mostly dry. However, the paper towel that is rolled up with the waxed paper will still be wet.

Now, you may be asking, "What does this have to do with plants in the desert?" Here's the answer: Cacti and other desert plants are like the paper towel that is rolled up with waxed paper. These plants have waxy coverings that keep moisture from evaporating into the dry desert air. That's part of the reason they can survive on the little water they get in the desert.

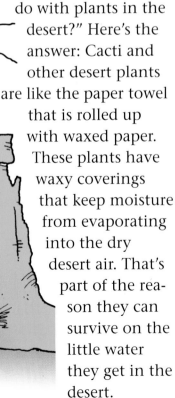

Colorful Carnation

*Do flowers ever get thirsty? In this project,
you can actually watch a flower "drink" water.*

What You'll Need:

white carnation

scissors or knife

two glasses

water

red and blue food coloring

GET A WHITE CARNATION with a long stem. With help from an adult, very carefully cut the carnation's stem lengthwise, from the bottom to about halfway up to the flower. Now fill two glasses with water. Use food coloring to color the water in one of the glasses dark red. Color the water in the other glass dark blue. Put the glasses right next to each other. Put one half of the carnation stem into each glass. Check the carnation a day later—and then two days later. Can you tell that the carnation has been drinking the water? You'll notice that the water travels up the tubes into the stem to reach the other parts of the plant.

Beautiful Bulbs

Brighten your winter by growing fresh spring flowers—indoors!

What You'll Need:

narcissus or hyacinth bulbs

shallow dish

pebbles or aquarium gravel

water

 NARCISSUS AND HYACINTH BULBS can be grown indoors using the technique called "forcing." To "force" a bulb, you trick it into thinking it's springtime.

Buy some paper-white narcissus bulbs or any type of hyacinth bulb at a garden store. Find a dish about three or four inches deep and pour in about 1 or 1½ inches of pebbles. Set three or four bulbs upright in the dish and fill in around them with more pebbles. Leave the tops of the bulbs sticking out. Add water up to the top of the pebbles. Set the dish in a cool, dark place for two weeks, adding water as needed, to allow roots to form. After two weeks, bring the dish out into a well-lit room, but out of direct light. When the leaves are well developed and flower buds are forming, set the dish in a sunny window. You can also try other spring flowers such as daffodils, crocus, or tulips.

Totally Tubular

Plants have two sets of tubes for transporting materials. The xylem brings water and minerals up the stem. The phloem brings nutrients from the leaves to the other parts of the plant.

Colors in a Leaf

Even green leaves have more colors than you may think!

What You'll Need:

coffee filter

scissors

leaves

coin

rubbing alcohol

jar

pencil

tape

aluminum foil

LEAVES HAVE A GREEN PIGMENT called chlorophyll that they use to capture sunlight. But did you know that leaves also have pigments of other colors to capture colors of light that chlorophyll misses? You can use chromatography to see the many colors in a leaf.

Cut a strip one inch wide from a coffee filter. Cut one end of the strip so that it is pointed. Place a leaf on the paper ¼ inch above the point. Roll the edge of a coin over the leaf, pressing green leaf juice into the paper. Let the paper dry. Then repeat the process with three different leaves.

Pour a ½-inch layer of rubbing alcohol into the bottom of a jar. Tape your paper strip to the middle of a pencil and hang it so that the very tip of the strip touches the alcohol. The colored strip of leaf "juices" should not touch the alcohol. You may have to adjust the length of the strip. Lay a piece of foil over the top of the jar to keep the alcohol from evaporating. Watch carefully as the alcohol moves up the filter paper, carrying the pigments along with it. In 10 to 20 minutes the colors should be separated. Do not allow them to run to the top of the paper. How many colors do you see? Could you see them in the leaf itself? The finished paper is called a chromatograph. Let it dry and use your chromatograph as a special bookmark.

Bark Rubbings

Tree bark and leaves have many interesting patterns that can be "collected" by making rubbings.

What You'll Need:

large crayon or colored chalk

thin paper

trees and leaves

hair spray

craft glue

notebook

pen

DO THIS PROJECT on a dry day, since wet tree bark will make your paper tear. Peel the paper from a large crayon, or use a thick piece of sidewalk chalk. Press a sheet of thin paper up against the bark of a tree. Gently rub the side of the crayon or chalk on the paper until the pattern of the bark shows. Compare rubbings from different trees. Which bark patterns make the nicest rubbings? Can you tell which rubbing came from which kind of tree? For leaf rubbings, lay the leaves flat on a hard, smooth surface. Cover the leaves with paper and rub the side of the crayon or chalk on the paper.

Ask an adult to spray the pictures with hair spray to keep the chalk from smearing. Glue your rubbings in a scrapbook to make a "Bark Book." Include some interesting facts about the trees.

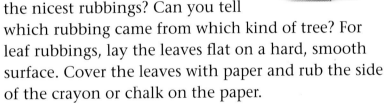

What Is Bark?

Bark is really the skin of the tree. It surrounds the trunk and branches to protect the tree. Trees grow wider each year, with the newest layer of wood growing right underneath the bark. Each tree has its own unique pattern of bark.

Grow a Tropical Tree

Enjoy a mango, papaya, or pomegranate. Then grow the tree it comes from!

What You'll Need:

tropical fruit pits
(from mango) or
seeds (from papaya
or pomegranate)

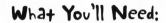

knife

vegetable brush

potting soil

flower pots

water

plastic wrap

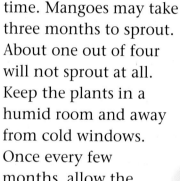

TROPICAL FRUIT PLANTS ARE FUN TO GROW, but it takes lots of patience. Getting them to sprout is the hardest part.

Mango: Begin with a very ripe mango. Have an adult help you cut the pit from the fruit and clean it with a vegetable brush under running water. Plant the flat pit in potting soil with one edge up. Cover it completely. Keep it watered, and wait a long time. Mangoes may take three months to sprout. About one out of four will not sprout at all. Keep the plants in a humid room and away from cold windows. Once every few months, allow the soil to go completely dry.

Papaya: Have an adult help you cut the fruit open and remove the small seeds from their fleshy coating (called an aril). Line the bottom of a flat dish with wet paper towels and lay the seeds on it. Cover with plastic wrap and set in a warm place. When the seeds just begin to sprout, rinse them in fresh water and plant in moist potting soil. Keep the seedlings out of direct sunlight until they are about 6 inches tall.

Pomegranate: Prepare and sprout the seeds as you did for papayas. Pomegranates are desert plants, so keep them in a dry room.

Chapter 3: Life in Other Kingdoms

BIOLOGISTS USED to classify life into just two kingdoms: plant and animal. However, they have realized that there are forms of life that aren't really plant or animal, so they created new kingdoms.

Fungi cannot make their own food; they grow on, and take their food from, living or dead organisms. You are probably familiar with some members of the fungus kingdom. Mushrooms are members of the fungus kingdom. Yeast, which makes bread dough rise, is also a fungus.

Common bacteria are single-cell organisms. Like fungi, bacteria cannot make their own food. They feed off other living things. But bacteria are in their own kingdom. Some bacteria cause diseases. Other bacteria are helpful, such as the bacteria that make yogurt.

Another little world, the protist kingdom, consists of many small organisms. Like animals, some of these organisms must eat other organisms to get their nutrients. Other protists, such as algae, are more like plants. They make their own nutrients through photosynthesis.

Viruses are tiny organisms that attack living cells. They don't move on their own or breathe, so many biologists do not consider them to be alive. Viruses infect plants and animals and cause disease.

Although a lot of these organisms are tiny, there is a lot you can learn about them in the projects and activities in this chapter.

Eat, Yeast, and Be Merry

This experiment is sure to get a rise out of you.

What You'll Need:

two glasses

dry yeast

measuring cup

measuring spoons

sugar

water

IN EACH OF TWO GLASSES, place ¼ teaspoon of dry yeast and 4 teaspoons of sugar. Add ¾ cup of cold water to one glass and ¾ cup of warm (not above 130°F) water to the other glass. Compare what happens to the yeast in the two glasses.

Was there a difference between the two glasses? With the aid of heat, the yeast in the warm cup was able to break down the sugar, giving off alcohol and a gas called carbon dioxide. The carbon dioxide bubbled up in the solution. Without the added heat, the yeast in the cold glass could not break down the sugar. When people bake bread, they add yeast to flour and put it in a warm place. The yeast breaks down sugar and releases carbon dioxide, which causes the bread dough to rise.

Yummy Yeast

Yeast are one-celled organisms. They are useful because they convert sugar into carbon dioxide and alcohol. Baking bread is just one of the ways yeast is used.

Down and Dirty

Tiny organisms keep changes occurring deep down in the earth.

What You'll Need:

garden soil

jar with a lid

small container

limewater, which is available at a drugstore

DROP A LARGE HANDFUL OF GARDEN SOIL into the bottom of a big empty jar. Pour some limewater into a small container. Note what the limewater looks like. Set the container of limewater, uncovered, inside the large jar so it rests on top of the soil. Tightly screw on the lid of the large jar, and leave it undisturbed. In two or three days, look at the limewater to see if it has changed in any way.

The soil contains many microscopic animals. These animals take in oxygen and release carbon dioxide as a waste product, just as you do when you breathe. The limewater turned a milky color because the carbon dioxide produced by the organisms in the soil combined with the limewater to produce chalk. Your garden soil may contain bacteria, protozoans, and threadlike worms called nematodes.

Moldy Oldy

Peanut butter and jelly on wheat, please. Hold the mold!

What You'll Need:

bread

resealable plastic bags

marker

napkins

water

BECAUSE BACTERIA CAN GROW IN FOOD, many companies add preservatives to their food products to slow or prevent the growth of bacteria. At your grocery store, purchase loaves of white and wheat bread that contain preservatives. Also find loaves of white and wheat bread that do not contain preservatives. At home, mark four resealable plastic bags as follows: "WHITE WITH PRESERVATIVES," "WHITE WITHOUT PRESERVATIVES," "WHEAT WITH PRESERVATIVES," and "WHEAT WITHOUT PRESERVATIVES." Moisten four paper napkins, and put one in each of the bags.

Slightly moisten one slice of each kind of bread, and put them in the appropriate bags. Put all four sealed bags on a plate next to one another, and set the plate in a warm, dark closet. Check your bread slices each day. Where does mold start growing first?

Well Fed on Bread

Bread mold makes enzymes that digest bread. Then the mold absorbs the nutrients. Like mushrooms, the mold creates spores in order to reproduce.

Break Down

What happens to grass clippings and raked leaves after you're done with the yard work? Try this activity to find out.

What You'll Need:

glass jar with a lid

fresh leaves

fresh grass cuttings

water

paper and pen

GATHER LEAVES AND GRASS CLIPPINGS, and pack them into a large clear jar. Add a few drops of water, and loosely screw the cap onto the jar. Be sure not to screw the cap tightly because gases will be given off that could break a tightly sealed jar.

Store the jar in a dark, warm place. Check on it every few days, and observe any changes. Write down your observations and the date each time you look at it.

What happened to the material in the jar? Microorganisms that feed on dead matter were able to grow in your jar. In feeding on the grass and leaves, they broke it down into a dark brown mixture that would, in the wild, become a part of the soil.

Nature's Secret

Nutrients cycle through nature. Decomposers break formerly living things down. Plants absorb these nutrients. Animals eat the plants. Then, when the animals die, the nutrients start the cycle again.

Spore Prints

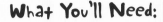

Did you know that mushooms can make their own prints?

What You'll Need:

mushrooms

white unlined index cards

black paper

drinking glass or bowl

hair spray or acrylic fixative

 FIND A MUSHROOM IN THE WILD, or get some from the store. (Be careful when handling wild mushrooms—and certainly don't eat them!) You will have to find some with the caps open. Look underneath the cap. The gills inside are lined with structures that make and release spores by the millions. Each spore can grow into a new fungus.

Cover half of an index card with black paper. Pop out the stem from the mushroom cap and place the cap on the card so that half is on the black paper and half on the white. Cover with a glass or bowl and let the cap sit overnight. The next day remove the glass and the mushroom cap. You should see a print of the mushroom spores. Pale spores will show up on the black paper, while darker ones will show on the white. Ask an adult to spray the print with hair spray or acrylic fixative to keep it from smearing.

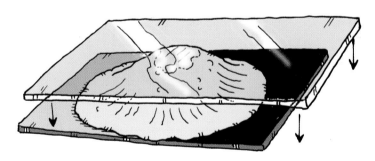

Decomposers

Is it the end or just the beginning? Find out when you watch decomposers do their work.

What You'll Need:

apple

IN NATURE, everything happens in cycles. For example, water moves in a cycle from rivers to oceans to clouds, back to the earth in the form of rain, which runs back into rivers, and so on. In this activity, you'll see part of the life cycle of plants. Decomposition is the last stage in the life cycle of a plant. But, in a way, it's also the first stage. That's how cycles work.

Take a few bites out of an apple. Put the apple outdoors in a damp area away from houses and people. It will also need to be a place where animals won't bother the apple. Leave the apple outside overnight.

The next day, take a look at the apple. Has it started to decompose? Do you see any decomposers at work? Decomposers are living things that break down the apple and turn it back into soil. Decomposers like flies and worms may be gross, but they're important!

Apples Anyone?

Did you know that there are over 2,500 varieties of apples produced in the United States? That means you could eat a different kind of apple every day for almost seven years!

The apple is made of elements such as carbon, hydrogen, oxygen, as well as others. It's no coincidence that soil is made of the same elements. Decomposers turn the apple back into soil, so new apples can grow. In fact, if no one disturbs your apple, and if the weather is right, the seeds in that apple just might sprout into new apple trees, putting down roots in soil that was once your apple. It's just one of nature's many cycles!

Chapter 4

Chemistry Connections

CHEMISTRY IS A BRANCH OF SCIENCE that studies matter—the stuff things are made from. Matter is made of molecules. Molecules are the smallest particles of a substance that still have the same properties as the original substance. A molecule is way too small to be seen with an unaided eye.

The way the molecules are arranged influences the properties of matter. These properties include volume, density, and how the molecule interacts with other molecules. Matter takes up space. The amount of space an object takes up is that object's volume. Density is how tightly packed the molecules are in an object. An object will float on a liquid if it is less dense than the liquid. It sinks if it is more dense than the liquid.

Molecules constantly interact with other molecules. Some of these interactions cause changes. When a change is temporary, it is called a physical change. Dissolving sugar into water is a physical change, because when the water evaporates, the sugar is left behind unchanged. When molecules interact and produce new molecules, a chemical change has taken place. Mixing vinegar and baking soda together produces carbon dioxide, a different molecule. Therefore, a chemical change has taken place.

Studying the world up close can help us understand it better. This chapter will help you to see why matter behaves like it does in its many forms.

Pop Up and Pop Down

Objects that look the same can have different densities.

What You'll Need:

bathtub

cans of soda

salt

FILL A BASIN, bathtub, aquarium, or other large container with water. Place several unopened cans of different kinds of soda into the water. Some of the cans will be heavier, or more dense, than water, and some will be less dense than water. The less dense cans will float, and the more dense cans will sink. Watch the cans, and note which ones float and which ones sink. What's the difference between the floaters and the sinkers? Do you think the cans are different or the soda is different? Can you form a hypothesis about which types of soda tend to sink and which types float? Use some other brands and types of soda to test your hypothesis.

If you add salt to the water, the water will become more dense. Can you predict how this might affect the cans of soda? Add salt to the water to see if your prediction was correct.

Floaters and Sinkers

The density of materials is often compared to water. Water has a density of one gram per cubic centimeter. If an object's density is greater than one, it will sink in water. If less than one, it will float in water.

Egg-citing Levitation

Why did the chicken make the egg float? To get to the other salt.

What You'll Need:

bowl

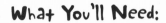
water

egg

salt

stirrer

FILL A CONTAINER with enough water to cover an egg. Place the egg in the water. Does the egg float or sink? The egg sinks because it is more dense than the water. Now add salt to the water, and stir gently, being careful not to break the egg. Keep adding salt until the egg floats. You will need about 4 tablespoons of salt for every 1½ cups of water.

Did the salt change the water's density? The liquids inside an egg are more dense than water so the egg usually sinks in water. Adding salt to water makes the water more dense. When enough salt is added, the egg will be less dense than the water. The egg will rise. You have produced the levitation of an egg!

Drop It—Slowly!

Water has different densities when it takes on other forms.
Try this test to see this fact in action.

What You'll Need:

bowl

corn oil

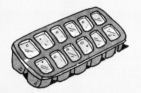

ice cube

HOT WATER IS LESS DENSE than cold water, but what about ice? The density of a substance changes depending on temperature because the volume of the substance changes with temperature. Volume is a measure of how much space a substance takes up, and as volume increases, density decreases.

Most often, things have a greater volume when they are warmer and a lesser volume when they are colder; the same amount of a substance will take up more space when it's warm than it

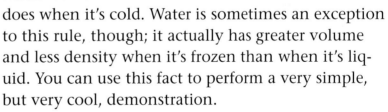

does when it's cold. Water is sometimes an exception to this rule, though; it actually has greater volume and less density when it's frozen than when it's liquid. You can use this fact to perform a very simple, but very cool, demonstration.

Fill a clear bowl halfway with corn oil, drop an ice cube in it, and sit back and watch. You'll notice right away that the ice cube floats on top of the oil. This is because the ice weighs less than the amount of oil needed to fill up the same volume. Eventually, the ice will melt and form drops of water. The liquid water has a lesser volume than the frozen water; the same amount takes up less space. This means that the liquid water is more dense than the frozen water; it is also more dense than the oil. The drops of water will form almost perfect spheres, and they will sink slowly to the bottom of the bowl.

Cabbage Patch Chemist

Is it an acid or a base? Would you believe that cabbage can tell you the answer?

What You'll Need:

purple cabbage

knife

pot

water

measuring cup

stove

strainer

jar

two clear cups

vinegar and clear ammonia

CHOP SOME PURPLE CABBAGE into small pieces. Put all of the pieces into a pot with 2 cups of water, and bring to a boil on the stove. Reduce the heat, and let the mixture simmer for 10 minutes. The water will turn purplish. Remove the pot from the heat. Allow the purplish liquid to cool. Strain the cabbage, and pour the liquid into a jar.

Pour some of the purple liquid into two clear cups. Pour a bit of vinegar into one cup, and note the color change. Pour a bit of ammonia into the other cup, and note the color change.

What happened? Vinegar is an acid. It caused the color of the cabbage juice to change from blue to a more reddish color. Ammonia is a weak base. It caused the color to change to green. Cabbage juice can be used to tell if chemicals are acids or bases.

Caution: *This project requires adult supervision.*

Gassy Acids

One unique fact about acids is that they all contain hydrogen. This is given off in the form of a gas whenever acids react with metal.

Milk It

Think that it's impossible? Now you can make water and oil mix.

What You'll Need:

two glass jars
with lids

vegetable oil

water

dishwashing liquid

FILL A GLASS JAR about one quarter of the way with vegetable oil. Pour in water until the jar is three quarters of the way full. Repeat with a second jar. Put lids on the jars securely, and shake them. The oil and water mix, but in time, the two liquids separate again, leaving the oil on top and water on the bottom. The oil floats because it is less dense than the water. Now add a squirt of dishwashing liquid to one of the jars. Shake both jars again.

Can you see a change? The detergent emulsifies the oil droplets, or breaks them into much smaller droplets. These small droplets remain suspended in the water and give the water a milky appearance. This kind of mixture is called an emulsion.

Doing the Dirty Work

Detergents are emulsifiers; they break large drops of oil into smaller droplets. This makes it easier to clean dishes and clothes.

Butter Me Up

Here's a new kind of trick: Make butter magically appear!

What You'll Need:

whipping cream

bowl

electric mixer or whisk

PUT A PINT OF WHIPPING CREAM into a bowl, and whip it. With an electric mixer on high speed, this will take seven to nine minutes; with a whisk, it will take longer. Eventually, you will see butter forming into a ball. Pour off the liquid, and taste the butter.

Milk contains fat, and whipping cream contains even more fat. This fat is broken into small droplets and dissolved in the water of milk to form an emulsion. The energy you added to the cream by beating it made the small droplets of fat crash into each other and form bigger drops. The larger drops crashed into each other and formed even larger drops, and so on, until you made one big drop of fat—butter. The process where small drops combine to form big drops is called coalescing.

Coalesce or Emulsify

Churning cream causes the oil molecules to coalesce or come together and this forms butter. To coalesce is the opposite of to emulsify. Both are physical—rather than chemical—changes.

Sweet Racers

Spread out some sugar molecules in this tasty test.

What You'll Need:

warm water

two glasses

sugar cubes

napkin

hammer

FILL TWO GLASSES halfway with warm water. Wrap a cube of sugar in a napkin. Use a hammer to gently break the sugar cube into tiny pieces of sugar. Drop a whole sugar cube into one glass of water and the crushed sugar cube into the second glass of water at the same time. In which glass does the sugar dissolve faster?

Sugar dissolves in water when the sugar molecules are surrounded by water molecules. In the glass with the crushed sugar cube, the water molecules were able to surround the sugar molecules and dissolve them faster because the sugar molecules were spread out.

Quick Reactions
The surface area to volume ratio is important in chemistry. More exposed surface area allows materials to dissolve or react faster.

Making a Density Column

See density illustrated before your very eyes.

What You'll Need:

cup   water

food coloring

spoon

narrow jar

turkey baster

corn syrup   glycerin

dishwashing liquid

vegetable oil

rubbing alcohol

various small objects

FILL A CUP with water, add some red food coloring, and stir. Set a tall, narrow jar on a table. Using a turkey baster, slowly add the following to the jar in this order: corn syrup, glycerin, dishwashing liquid, colored water, vegetable oil, and rubbing alcohol. Add enough of each to fill about one sixth of the jar. When you add each substance, put the tip of the baster on the side of the jar, and squeeze the bulb gently so the liquid slides down the side of the jar. Don't squirt it in. The liquids you've added will stay separate from each other; the less dense liquids will float on top of the more dense liquids. Take a cork, a marble, a paper clip, and several other small objects, and add them one at a time to the jar. The objects will float at different levels. Can you guess why?

Making a Hydrometer

Discover different densities with this homemade device.

What You'll Need:

two glasses

water

salt

measuring cup

spoon

plastic drinking straw

scissors

plasticine clay

string

FILL TWO GLASSES with water. Add ⅓ cup of salt to one of the glasses of water, and stir it with a spoon. Set both glasses on a counter while you make your hydrometer.

Cut a plastic drinking straw so that it's a little longer than your glass. Put a small ball of plasticine clay about the size of a marble at the end of the straw. Be sure that the clay makes a tight fit on the straw so that water won't leak into the straw.

Put the clay end of the straw into the glass of plain water; it should float just off the bottom. If it doesn't float, remove a little of the clay. When your straw and clay float, take the straw out of the water, and tie a piece of string around the middle of the straw. Put the straw back in the water. Slide the string to mark the water level on the straw. The straw is now a hydrometer. The higher the straw floats in a glass of liquid, the denser the liquid is.

Put your hydrometer into the glass of salt water. Where is the string? Use your hydrometer to check the density of other liquids, such as cooking oil or milk.

Marbles in Water

Pump up the volume without worrying about being too loud.

What You'll Need:

water

2-cup measuring cup

16 marbles of the same size

paper and pen

AN OBJECT'S VOLUME determines how much space it takes up. Try this activity to see how it works.

Pour 1 cup of water into a 2-cup measuring cup. Drop four marbles into the water. What is the water level in the measuring cup now? Write this down. Drop four more marbles into the water. What is the level of the water in the measuring cup now? Could you predict, using the information that you have written down, what the level of water will be when you add eight more marbles? Write down your prediction. Add eight more marbles to the cup of water. Was your prediction correct?

What's the Volume?

Volume is the amount of space an object takes up. You can measure an object's volume by seeing how much water it displaces. Or, if the object is a rectangle, volume can be calculated by multiplying its length by its width by its height.

Flame Out

Investigate the densities of gases in this hot experiment.

What You'll Need:

cardboard tube from a roll of wrapping paper

knife

candle   candleholder

matches

glass

baking soda

measuring spoon

vinegar

CUT A 10-INCH SECTION of cardboard tube from a roll of wrapping paper. Put a candle in a candleholder in a safe place on a table. Light the candle. Put 1 teaspoon of baking soda into an empty glass. Add 1 inch of vinegar to the glass. You will see bubbles forming. These bubbles contain carbon dioxide gas, which is formed as the vinegar and baking soda mix together. Hold up the cardboard tube, and tip it down toward the candle flame, but don't get it too close or it will burn. Carefully pour the bubbles from the glass into the tube and toward the flame without getting liquid into the flame. Observe what happens to the flame.

What happened to the flame? As you poured the bubbles into the tube, the carbon dioxide gas traveled down the tube and came out the other end, covering the flame and keeping oxygen from it. The flame went out. This happens because carbon dioxide is heavier than air.

Caution: *This project requires adult supervision.*

Carbon Dioxide Is All Right!

This gas really gets around. It is part of the air we breathe as well as an ingredient in carbonated soda pop. Carbon dioxide is even used in some fire extinguishers.

Grow a Crystal "Garden"

At one time, these were called "Depression gardens" because they were an inexpensive project for children during the Great Depression of the 1930s.

What You'll Need:

chunks of coal

brick

flower pot pieces

old shallow bowls about 6 inches wide

mixing bowl

salt (not iodized)

liquid bluing and ammonia

water

food coloring

REMEMBER TO BE CAREFUL when working with any broken objects and when pouring ammonia. Have an adult supervise this project.

Break coal, brick, clay flower pots, or unglazed porcelain into chunks the size of walnuts. Place several in an old dish, clustering them near the center. (Don't overcrowd the dish.) For each dish, mix four tablespoons of salt (not iodized), four tablespoons of liquid bluing, four tablespoons of water, and one tablespoon of household ammonia. Pour the mixture very slowly over the broken pieces in your dish. Drip food coloring on the pieces sticking up out of the solution. Set the bowl aside in a place it won't be disturbed. In a few hours you should see crystals "growing" in your garden.

To make crystal blossoms: Make a larger batch of the solution given above but leave out the ammonia. Make enough to completely cover the broken pieces in the dish (keep the pile low, under the rim of the dish). Add more solution every day or two to keep the same liquid level. After two weeks stop adding solution and allow the liquid to evaporate completely. Beautiful blossom shapes will form.

Sweet Crystals

In this activity, you'll do two things at once:
see how crystals form in nature and make candy!

What You'll Need:

saucepan

water

sugar

glass jar

string

pencil

Popsicle stick

WITH THE HELP OF AN ADULT, boil ½ cup of water in a saucepan. Add 1 cup of sugar one spoonful at a time until all the sugar is dissolved. Keep adding sugar until the solution turns into a clear syrup. Let it cool for about ten minutes, then pour the syrup into a glass jar.

Now get a piece of string about six inches long. Tie one end of the string around a pencil. Then tie the other end to a Popsicle stick. Put the pencil on top of the jar so the Popsicle stick hangs in the syrup.

Set your "crystal maker" aside. Take a look at it every day to see what's happening. In about a week, the syrup should be crystallized and ready to eat.

Chapter 5

Moving Experiences

WHILE AT A PICNIC in the park, you hear a roar and look up to the sky and see an airplane flying overhead. Then, out of the corner of your eye, you see a crawling crouton. You turn and look to see an ant carrying away a huge crumb. From airplanes to ants, moving things always attract our attention.

The ant and the airplane use energy to move. The ant's energy comes from the food it eats. The airplane's energy is from the kerosene it burns. The energy creates a force that creates motion. The ant's legs propel it forward, and the jet engines propel the jet forward.

This illustrates one of Sir Isaac Newton's laws of motion: For every action there is an equal and opposite reaction. The burning kerosene pushes hot gases out of the jet engine (the action). This causes the airplane to be pushed forward (the reaction). Motion can also be caused by gravity. When we drop a ball, it falls because of the earth's gravity.

All of this constant motion can seem pretty chaotic. But this chapter's projects and activities are sure to get you moving in the right direction!

Wing It

This activity reveals one of the secrets of how planes fly.

What You'll Need:

paper

scissors

DANIEL BERNOULLI, a Swiss scientist, discovered in 1738 that moving air has less pushing power than still air. This idea, called Bernoulli's principle, is used in the design of airplanes.

To demonstrate the principle, cut a strip of paper 2 inches wide and about 8 inches long. Hold one corner of a 2-inch side of the strip in each hand, and hold it just below your lower lip. Gently blow across the strip of paper. You will see that the paper rises.

The air you blow over the top of the paper is moving air, so it has less pushing power. The air pressure underneath the strip remains normal. The strong air pressure underneath pushes up and causes the strip of paper to lift. Wings of airplanes are shaped with curved tops to make the air move fast, and the fast-moving air along the top of the wing reduces air pressure and causes "lift," an upward force that opposes gravity.

Airborne Forces

There are four forces that act on an airplane when it is in flight. These are thrust, drag, lift, and weight. These forces work against each other to keep the plane up. The thrust of the engines works against the drag of the air resistance, and the lift of the wings works against the gravitational weight of the plane.

Parachute Power

Take a look at how parachutes work with this airborne activity.

What You'll Need:

paper

scissors

ruler

tape

string

paper clips

CUT TWO 12-INCH SQUARES and two 8-inch squares of paper. Securely tape 10-inch pieces of string to all four corners of all four pieces of paper. Gather the four strings from one square of paper, and tie them to a paper clip. Repeat with the other three squares.

Drop an 8-inch "parachute" and a 12-inch "parachute" at the same time from a staircase, porch, or deck. Make sure you drop the parachutes from the same height. Which reaches the ground last, the big or the small parachute? Add three more paper clips to one of the 8-inch parachutes. Drop both 8-inch parachutes. Which one reaches the ground first? Put a small hole in the middle of one 12-inch parachute. Drop both 12-inch parachutes. Which one reaches the ground first?

You will find that the more surface area your parachute has, the slower it will fall. The larger surface encounters more air molecules as it falls, making it fall slower. A parachute with a heavier load falls faster because the force of gravity working against the air resistance is greater.

Word Origins

Did you know that the word "parachute" comes from the French? *Parer* means "to avoid" and *chute* means "a fall."

Journey to the Center of Gravity

Get centered in order to get a grip on gravity.

What You'll Need:

paper clip

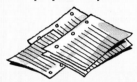

notebook paper

pencil

tape

BEND A PAPER CLIP OPEN to make an "L" shape. Put the tip of the short side of the paper clip on the tip of your index finger, and try to balance it. The paper clip will fall off. Take a half sheet of notebook paper, and roll it into a small tube around a pencil. Use tape at both ends of the paper to keep the tube from unrolling. Remove the pencil.

Tape the end of the long side of the paper clip to the end of the tube of paper. Now try to balance the paper clip on your index finger.

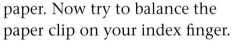

What caused the change here? By adding more weight to the bottom of the paper clip, you changed the paper clip's center of gravity—the point where the force of gravity is equal on either side. That allowed you to balance the clip on your finger in a way that you were not able to do before.

Center Yourself

A low center of gravity is important in sports such as wrestling and football and in many of the martial arts. You can lower your center of gravity by bending your knees and crouching slightly. This makes you more stable.

High Bounce

In this activity, what goes down, must come up.

What You'll Need:

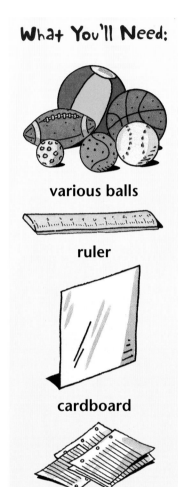

various balls

ruler

cardboard

paper

pen

COLLECT SOME DIFFERENT BALLS (tennis ball, beach ball, softball, rubber ball, football, basketball, golf ball, etc.). Make a graph that has the names of the different balls across the bottom and height (of each ball's bounce) in feet along the sides.

Test the different balls to see which one bounces best on a concrete floor, porch, or driveway. Drop them one at a time from the same height in front of a large sheet of cardboard, and mark on the cardboard how high each one bounced. Then, measure each bounce and indicate it on your graph.

All the balls gained the same amount of energy when they fell. When they struck the ground, the downward force of gravity was converted into energy that bounced the ball up in the air. The different materials and sizes of the balls affected how well each one could convert the energy of gravity into the energy of the bounce (how high each ball bounced).

Darn Tootin' it Was Newton!

It may seem obvious now, but in 1687, Sir Isaac Newton was the first person to show that the harder a stone is thrown, the farther it will travel before gravity forces it back down to the ground. This principle eventually led to the launching of satellites into space—almost 300 years later!

Target Practice

Bean bag tossing takes a tricky turn when motion and gravity are part of the game.

What You'll Need:

black paper

ruler

scissors

bean bag

bicycle

CHALLENGE A FRIEND to target practice. From a sheet of black paper, cut out two black circles. Make a 1-inch-diameter circle and a 6-inch-diameter circle.

In a safe place, take turns with your friend riding past the target on your bike and trying to drop a bean bag on the target as you go by without stopping. Be careful to watch where you are going as you try to hit the target! After several tries, you'll learn when to drop the bean bag. Do you drop it when you are directly over the target? You'll find that the bean bag is moving just as much as you are moving. And a moving object will keep moving at a constant speed as gravity pulls it down. When you and your friend can hit the 6-inch target, try the 1-inch target.

Snap That Seat Belt!

If you are in a car going 60 mph, you are also going 60 mph. If the car suddenly stops, your body still moves forward at 60 mph. Therefore, if you didn't have a seat belt on, you could get hurt as your body moves forward into the front seat (if you're sitting in back) or windshield. So always buckle up!

Water Pressure Gauge

Gravity works its force on everything on earth.
In this project, gravity puts the pressure on water.

What You'll Need:

pencil

½-gallon container

tape

water

sink

ruler

USE A PENCIL POINT to poke three holes on one side of an empty ½-gallon container, one directly above the other. One hole should be 1 inch from the bottom of the container; the middle hole should be 3 inches above the first; and the third hole should be 3 inches above the middle hole.

Put a piece of tape down the side of the container to cover up the three holes. Fill the carton with water, and set it in the sink. Pull off the piece of tape, and watch the water flow from the holes. You'll see that the water shoots out the greatest distance from the bottom hole and the least distance from the top hole. You'll also see that the water from each hole squirts less and less far as time passes.

As gravity pulls down on the water, the water exerts a downward force that we call "water pressure." The more water you have, the greater the amount of downward force it will produce. The force of water pressure that made the water squirt out of the holes was stronger at the bottom of the carton than at the top because the bottom had more water above it pressing down. That's why the water squirted farther from the bottom hole. As the water drained from the carton, the to water pressure decreased, and the water didn't squirt as far.

Flyin' Through the Xylem

One way pressure seems to defy gravity is in the internal transport system of plants (the xylem). Water and nutrients are absorbed by the plant's roots. Then pressure moves the liquid up through the stem to nourish all the parts of the plant.

Pendulum Patterns

Patterns are revealed throughout the study of science. Here you can catch a glimpse of the pattern of a swinging pendulum.

What You'll Need:

two chairs

dark paper

broom

paper cup

string

tape

salt

ruler

STAND TWO CHAIRS ABOUT 3 FEET APART, and cover the area between the chairs with a large piece of dark paper. Lay a broom handle across the backs of the chairs. Poke a small hole in the bottom of a paper cup. Tape a 6-inch string to the paper cup on either side to form a handle. Tie the handle of the paper cup to a 3-foot piece of string, and then tie the string to the middle of the broom handle between the two chairs.

Hold your finger over the hole in the bottom of the paper cup, and fill the cup with salt. Then pull the cup toward one of the corners of the sheet of dark paper. Release both your finger and the cup. The cup will swing like a pendulum in a pattern, and you will be able to see the pattern it swings in by observing the salt that drops onto the paper.

Swinging Together

You can see that motion can transfer from one moving object to another in this exercise.

What You'll Need:

two chairs

string

two paper cups

marbles

ruler

PLACE TWO CHAIRS ABOUT 4 FEET APART. Tie a string between the backs of the chairs. Punch two holes opposite one another in the lip of a paper cup. Thread a 4-inch string through the holes, and tie a knot to make a handle for the cup. Repeat this process with a second cup. Tie a 2-foot-long piece of string to the handle of each cup. Tie the free ends of the strings to the string stretched between the two chairs; tie the strings so they are about 1 foot apart. Put two marbles in each cup. Hold one cup to the side, and then release it. Watch as it begins to swing. What happens to the other cup? Put four marbles in one cup and two in the other. What happens if the heavy cup is put in motion first? The light cup?

Sound Resonance

The movement of one object can affect the movement of a connected object. This is called "resonance." If you strike a tuning fork (used to tune musical instruments or voices), causing it to vibrate, and hold it next to an identical tuning fork, it will also begin to vibrate.

Whirligig

Whether we notice them or not, forces are active all around us. Gravity and magnetism are two forces. Here we take a look at centrifugal force.

What You'll Need:

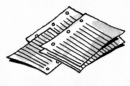

paper

string

tape

cardboard toilet paper tube

TAKE A HALF SHEET OF NOTEBOOK PAPER, and wad it up into a small ball. Stick the end of a 2-foot piece of string into the ball of paper, and tape it to the paper. Thread the string through a cardboard tube from an empty roll of toilet paper. Wad a full sheet of paper into a tight ball. Stick the other end of the piece of string into the large ball of paper, and tape it to the paper. Let the small ball stick out of the tube about 5 inches at the top, while the large ball hangs down from the bottom. Grasp the tube in one hand, and move your hand in a small circular motion so that the small ball spins around the tube. Spin it faster and faster, and watch the large ball begin to rise. Continue moving your hand, and pull down on the large ball. Watch what happens to the speed of the small ball.

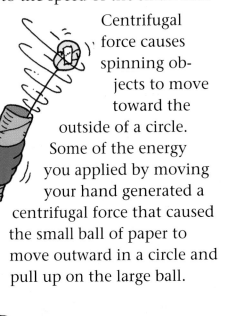

Centrifugal force causes spinning objects to move toward the outside of a circle. Some of the energy you applied by moving your hand generated a centrifugal force that caused the small ball of paper to move outward in a circle and pull up on the large ball.

Pulley Power

Avoid too much lifting grief and let a pully give you some relief.

What You'll Need:

empty 1-quart milk carton

marbles

scissors

string

metal coat hanger

wire cutters

empty spool

dowel

books

OPEN THE FLAPS of an empty 1-quart milk carton, and put 24 marbles inside. Close the carton, and punch a hole through the top with scissors. Push a 3-inch piece of strong string through the hole, and tie the string in a knot to form a loop. Take a coat hanger, and use wire cutters to carefully cut off the long, straight piece on the bottom. (Save this to use in Using a Roller on page 77.) Bend the two short arms of the coat hanger through the hole in the center of a spool of thread until the ends of the arms touch each other. Put the hook of the coat hanger through the loop of string you tied to the milk carton.

Set a dowel on a table so it extends 6 inches over the side of the table; set some heavy books on top of the dowel to hold it in place. Place the milk carton on the floor beneath the dowel.

First lift the milk carton 6 inches off the floor by holding the carton by the flaps and pulling it up in your hands. Now tie one end of a 5-foot piece of string to the dowel. Pass the other end of the string under the spool of thread. Lift the carton of marbles about 6 inches off the floor by pulling the string 12 inches. The milk carton will feel only half as heavy as it did before; pulling the string twice the distance that you raise the carton means you need to exert only half the force to lift it.

Using a Roller

Using a ramp can really help get a job rolling!

What You'll Need:

books

ruler

thin metal rod
(see page 76)

empty spool

string

toy car   marbles

empty margarine tub

paper and pen

cardboard

PUT TWO STACKS OF BOOKS, 9 inches apart, at the edge of a table. Each stack should be 9 inches tall and placed so that part of each stack of books sticks out over the edge of the table. Place a thin metal rod through an empty spool of thread, and rest the rod across the stack of books. Add a few more books to each stack to hold the rod in place. Tie a 2-foot piece of string to the front of a toy car. Put the car on the table beneath the rod, and put the other end of the piece of string up over the spool of thread.

Punch two holes opposite each other in the rim of an empty margarine tub. Tie an 8-inch piece of string through the holes to form a handle for the tub. Tie the other end of the string that is attached to the toy car to the handle of your tub.

Add marbles to the margarine tub, one at a time, until there is enough weight to lift the toy car 5 inches into the air. Empty the tub, and count the marbles. Write the number down.

Add a third stack of books, 5 inches high, between the other two stacks. Use a sturdy piece of cardboard to make a ramp between the top of the middle stack of books and the table. Put the toy car at the bottom of the ramp.

Put marbles, one by one, into the tub until there's enough weight to pull the toy car to the top of the ramp. Empty the tub, and count the marbles. Write the number down. Using a ramp to help, did it take more or less weight to lift the toy car?

Blast Off

According to one of Sir Isaac Newton's laws of motion,
for every action there is an equal and opposite reaction.

What You'll Need:

two 3-foot dowels

hammer   fishing line

drinking straw

empty plastic
screw-top bottle

vinegar   tape

baking soda

measuring spoon

tissue paper

CAREFULLY POUND TWO 3-FOOT DOWELS into the ground about 6 feet apart. Tie a 7-foot piece of fishing line to one dowel, thread the loose end through a drinking straw, and then tie the other end to the second dowel, stretching the string tightly between the dowels.

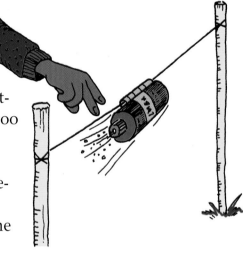

Put a hole through the cap of an empty plastic screw-top bottle, such as a shampoo bottle. Remove the cap from the bottle. Pour an inch of vinegar into the bottle. Tape the bottle to the straw on the fishing line so the bottle is horizontal. Slide the bottle along the fishing line all the way to one end so that the cap is next to the dowel.

Put 3 teaspoons of baking soda into a small piece of tissue paper. Roll the paper up, slip it into the bottle, and quickly screw the cap back on the bottle.

Carefully shake the bottle back and forth for a few seconds, and then let go of the bottle. The bottle will travel the length of the fishing line, propelled like a rocket.

The baking soda and vinegar produced carbon dioxide gas when they were mixed together. The gas was forced out of the hole in the bottle cap. As the gas pushed backward out of the bottle, it exerted an equal force in the opposite direction, which propelled the bottle forward.

Water-powered Boat

This homemade boat doesn't need a motor or sails in order to make it go.

What You'll Need:

knife

empty 1-quart milk carton

pencil

paper cup

bendable drinking straw

CAREFULLY CUT AN EMPTY 1-quart milk carton in half lengthwise. You only need one half, so set the other half aside. Set your half down on the table so you can see the inside of the carton. The top of the milk carton will be the bow, or front, of your boat, and the bottom will be the stern, or the back. Using a pencil, make a hole just big enough for a drinking straw to fit, near the bottom and in the center of the boat's stern.

Poke a hole of the same size in the side of a paper cup ½-inch up from the bottom. Bend a bendable drinking straw into an "L" shape. Put the long end of the straw through the hole in the boat's stern. Now put the short end of the straw through the hole in the cup, and set the cup inside the boat.

Fill your bathtub or sink with water, and put the boat in it. Be sure that the straw poking out from the boat is below the water's surface. Hold a finger over the end of the straw in the paper cup while you fill the cup with water. Take your finger off the straw, and watch your boat move.

Gravity made the water flow out of the cup, through the straw, and into the sink. As it was forced out of the straw, the water exerted an equal force in the opposite direction, which propelled the boat forward.

Chapter 6: Energizing Experiences

CAN YOU IMAGINE what it would be like on earth if someone destroyed all the energy? In the last chapter you learned that energy can cause objects to move. Imagine if there were no flying birds, jumping frogs, or swaying trees.

Magnetism is another form of energy. If energy disappeared, magnets would not attract or repel and compasses wouldn't point north. Electricity is also a type of energy. Imagine what it would be like without any electric lamps, heaters, or televisions.

The light from the sun is also energy. If the sun's energy ran out, it would be totally dark. Plants would not be able to make food. Heat is energy. Without energy, it would be terribly cold. Even sound is a form of energy.

Energy is vital to our life. Our world would be a very different place without it. Fortunately, it is impossible to destroy energy. Energy can only be converted from one form into another.

This chapter will ground you in energy and its many forms. Although these exciting projects may not shock you, you're sure to get a charge out of them!

Make Your Own Rainbow

Light may look white but it is actually made up of a rainbow of colors.

What You'll Need:

shallow pan

water

mirror

white paper

WITH A LITTLE PATIENCE, you will be able to make your own rainbow. Fill a pan with water, and place it on a table right in front of a sunny window. Now put a small mirror in the pan of water at the end of the pan. Slant the mirror so that it is facing the window.

Next, hold a sheet of white paper between the window and the pan of water. Slowly tilt the mirror back and forth to catch the light at different angles as it passes through the water and hits the mirror. The light will reflect from the mirror and pass through the water. As it passes through the water, it will bend. If you angle the mirror in just the right way, the light will bend enough to make a rainbow that will show up on the paper. Be patient and keep trying; sometimes it can take a while.

Prisms

Here's another way to sneak a peek at the rainbow that lives in light.

What You'll Need:

cardboard

scissors

prism

white paper

CUT A SLIT IN A LARGE PIECE OF CARDBOARD. Place the cardboard in a sunny window so that a shaft of sunlight shines through the slit. In one hand, hold a prism in front of the cardboard so that the sunlight passes through it. With your other hand, hold a sheet of white paper so that the light passing through the prism shines on it. You will see a rainbow of colors on the paper.

Raindrop Prisms

Rainbows form when raindrops act like a prism. Whenever you see a rainbow, the sun is shining from behind you.

Color Mix-up

Instead of separating colors from white light, this activity combines colors to make white. It's like a reverse rainbow!

What You'll Need:

three flashlights

cellophane in red, blue, and yellow

rubber bands

white paper

COVER THE LENS OF A FLASHLIGHT with red cellophane, and hold the cellophane in place with a rubber band. Cover the lens of a second flashlight with blue cellophane, and hold it in place with a rubber band. Cover the lens of a third flashlight with yellow cellophane, and secure it with a rubber band.

Set a sheet of white paper on the floor. Darken the room. Shine the red flashlight on the paper, and you will see a red spot. Shine the blue flashlight on the paper, and you'll see a blue spot. The yellow flashlight will produce a yellow spot.

Now overlap the spots of light from the yellow and blue flashlights; you will see a green spot. Ask a friend to shine the red light on your green spot, and the light will be almost white. The colors of the spectrum produce white light when mixed together.

Primary Colors

Actually, you can mix just three colors to produce white light: red, green, and violet blue. These three colors are called the primary colors. Various combinations of the primary colors produce all of the other colors of the spectrum.

Colors at a Distance

Such factors as lighting and distance make certain colors easier to see than others. Try it for yourself!

What You'll Need:

hanger

strips of cloth

paper and pen

ASK A FRIEND to tie narrow strips of different-colored cloth to the bottom of a coat hanger so that the strips hang down neatly. Have your friend hang the coat hanger on a tree limb some distance from you.

Divide a sheet of paper into two columns. Write your name at the top of one column and your friend's name at the top of the other column. Down the left side, list the colors of your strips of cloth: yellow, orange, red, green, blue, black, and so on. When your friend says that the coat hanger is ready to be viewed, carry the sheet of paper and your pen, and walk toward the strips of cloth. As soon as you can see a color, write the number "1" on the paper under your name and next to the color you see to indicate that you saw that color first. Continue numbering all the colors as you see them. Now let your friend have a turn. Do you both agree on which color you were able to see first? Try the experiment again at a different time of day when the light is different. Compare your results to your first experiment.

Fire Engine...Green?

Fire trucks used to be painted red until scientists discovered that red was harder to see at a distance than some other colors. Now many fire trucks are painted a light green color because it is very easy to see.

Black to Colors

*Reveal the fact that black isn't just black
but a whole bunch of colors rolled into one!*

What You'll Need:

paper towels

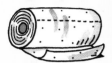

scissors

pencil

tape

glass

black marker

rubbing alcohol

TAKE A WHITE PAPER TOWEL, and cut a strip 2 inches wide. Tape the strip to a pencil, and lay the pencil across the rim of a glass so the paper towel hangs into the glass. Cut the paper towel so that the bottom of it just touches the bottom of the glass as it hangs from the pencil.

Draw a ¼-inch stripe on the paper towel about 1½ inches from the loose end with a black felt-tip marker.

Pour 1 inch of rubbing alcohol into the glass. Set the pencil on top of the glass so that the towel is in the alcohol and the black ink line is above the alcohol. Let the materials sit for an hour, checking them now and then. Do you see any colors besides black on the paper towel?

The color in the marker's ink was created by combining several other colors. As the alcohol was absorbed by the paper towel and traveled upward, it took some of the ink with it. It carried the different colors different distances, so they appeared in layers on the paper towel above the black line.

Chromatography

Chemists use a process called chromatography to separate materials. In paper chromatography, a liquid dissolves some materials more than others and some materials stick to the paper more than others.

Shadow Clock

Explore the case of the moving shadow.

What You'll Need:

chalk

watch or clock

ON A SUNNY MORNING, draw an arrow with chalk on your patio or driveway. Ask a friend to stand facing in the direction of the arrow with one foot on either side of the arrow. Now trace around your friend's shadow with chalk. Is it a long or short shadow? Is it in front of your friend or behind your friend? Inside the shadow, write down the time.

Every two hours, ask your friend to come back and stand in the same spot. Each time, trace around your friend's shadow, and write the time inside this shadow.

At the end of the day, look at the shadow tracings. Why are some shadows in front of where your friend stood and some behind? Why are some shadows small and some long? Think about where the sun is in the sky at different times of the day.

Me and My Shadow

When the sun is directly overhead, your shadow is smallest. When the sun is more toward the east or the west, your shadow becomes longer.

Hot, Hotter, Hottest

Some colors and materials are better at reflecting the heat of the sun than others.

What You'll Need:

four resealable plastic storage bags

water

white, orange, and black construction paper

aluminum foil

thermometer

paper and pen

FILL FOUR RESEALABLE PLASTIC STORAGE BAGS with water, and seal them tightly. Place the bags outside in a sunny spot on the sidewalk, driveway, or patio where they will not be disturbed. Wrap one bag in a sheet of white construction paper, one in a sheet of orange construction paper, one in a sheet of black construction paper, and one in a sheet of aluminum foil. Predict what effect the different wrappings will have on how the sun's energy heats the water in each bag. Which will be the warmest? Which will be the coolest? Using a thermometer, measure the temperature of the water in each bag after an hour. Were your predictions correct?

Reflect on This

When light hits a black object, all of the light is absorbed and none is reflected. When light hits a white object, all the light is reflected. This is why black objects get hotter in the sun than white objects.

A Kaleidoscope

Everything looks topsy-turvy in this test of reflection.

What You'll Need:

three small mirrors of the same size

tape

waxed paper

pencil

scissors

construction paper

To MAKE A KALEIDOSCOPE, tape together three small mirrors in a triangle shape, with the mirror sides facing inward. Stand the mirrors up on a piece of waxed paper, and trace around the bottom of the mirrors. Cut out this triangle shape, and then tape the piece of waxed paper in place at the bottom of the three mirrors. Cut out many small pieces and shapes from colored sheets of construction paper, and drop them inside the mirrors. Give your kaleidoscope a shake, then look inside. You will see some interesting patterns. The mirrors will reflect fascinating shapes and colors.

Identical Angles

A ray of light, when it hits a mirror, bounces off (or reflects). The angle that the ray of light comes in on will be the same angle that the ray is reflected.

Bouncing Cereal

Make objects jump at your thunderous command!

What You'll Need:

plastic wrap

metal bowl

rubber band

cereal flakes

cookie sheet

spoon

STRETCH A PIECE OF PLASTIC WRAP tightly over the top of a metal bowl. Secure it in place with a tight rubber band. Put a small handful of cereal flakes on top of the plastic wrap. Stand near the bowl, and loudly bang a cookie sheet with a spoon. Watch the cereal flakes.

What happened to the cereal? Striking the cookie sheet produced sound waves—vibrations—that traveled through the air. When the vibrations struck the plastic wrap, it vibrated, too, and that caused the cereal to move.

Invisible Waves

A loud sound causes air molecules to be pushed away. These air molecules push other air molecules, which in turn push other air molecules. This creates a sound wave that travels to your ears, making your eardrums vibrate.

Frying Pan Chimes

Sound waves can pass from one object to another and can even be amplified!

What You'll Need:

string

scissors

tape

frying pan

silverware

CUT FIVE PIECES OF STRING, each about 15 inches long. Tie the end of a piece of string just beneath the tines of a fork. Tape the string inside a frying pan, on the side directly opposite the handle. Repeat this process with other pieces of silverware. When you hold the frying pan by its handle, the silverware will dangle down on strings and bang into one another. Shake the pan, and listen to the sound it produces.

When the silverware pieces struck each other, they vibrated. The vibrations from each piece traveled up the strings at the same time and caused the pan to vibrate. The large pan amplified (made the sounds louder) the combined vibrations and produced the sounds.

Sympathetic Vibrations

We can't see the sound waves, but we can see their effect.

What You'll Need:

two identical wine glasses

water

pencil

short piece of fine wire

POUR WATER INTO A WINE GLASS until it is one third of the way full. Tap the side with a pencil. It will make a musical sound. By adding more or less water, you can change the sound. The tapping causes the side of the glass to vibrate. (Some wine glasses are delicate. Always be careful when working with glass.)

Pour exactly the same amount of water into a second wine glass. When you tap both glasses with a pencil, they will give the same sound. If there is a difference in the sound, add a little water to one glass until they do make the same sound. Stand the water glasses on a table about 4 inches apart. Place a piece of fine wire across the top of the glass that is farthest from you. Strike the closest glass, and watch the wire on the other glass. It will move slightly. The wire responds to your tapping on the other glass because the glasses vibrate in sympathy. If you continue to tap, the wire on the far glass will gradually move enough to fall.

Rubber Bands

Make a cardboard box guitar to see how different vibrations create different sounds.

What You'll Need:

cardboard box

three long rubber bands

 STRETCH THREE RUBBER BANDS around a small, sturdy cardboard box that is about 8 inches square and 2 inches deep. Space the rubber bands about 2 inches apart.

Pluck each of the rubber bands. Do they make a sound? Do they sound alike? Pull the middle rubber band tighter, and tie a knot to shorten it a little. Pull one of the other rubber bands very tight, and tie a knot to shorten it. Pluck the rubber bands again. Which one produces the highest sound? Which one produces the lowest sound?

By pulling the rubber bands tighter, you changed the rate at which they vibrate. The change in vibration rate caused a change in the sound they made.

Reflecting Sound

You can use umbrellas to help sound travel long distances.

What You'll Need:

two umbrellas

two pieces of sturdy, bendable wire

a watch that ticks loudly

tape

LAY TWO OPEN UMBRELLAS on the ground about 2 yards apart (1 yard is equal to 3 feet). The handles should face each other. Twist the middle of a piece of sturdy, bendable wire around the handle of one umbrella. Push both ends of the wire into the ground to support the umbrella so that it is horizontal with the ground. Repeat with the other umbrella.

Move a ticking watch along the handle of one umbrella to find the spot where the ticking sounds loudest. Tape the watch in place at that spot. Now move to the other umbrella, and hold your ear to the corresponding spot on the umbrella handle. You should be able to hear the watch.

The sound of the watch strikes the inside of the umbrella it's attached to and bounces off of it. The sound waves then strike the inside of the other umbrella and bounce off at the same angle. The shape of the umbrella focuses the sound waves at a single point along the handle.

An Electromagnet

Making your own magnet is easy with iron and electricity.

What You'll Need:

iron bolt

electrical wire

6-volt battery with screw-down terminals

various household objects

WIND A 3-FOOT PIECE OF ELECTRICAL WIRE around a long iron bolt about 20 times; make the loops close together, and leave about 10 inches of wire loose on each side of the coil. Connect the two loose ends of the wire to a 6-volt battery. The bolt is now an electromagnet and will attract metal containing iron. Test the electromagnet using paper clips, spoons, and other household items to see how strong it is. Disconnect the wire from the battery, and see if the magnet still works.

As electricity from the battery flowed through the wire, it caused the molecules in the bolt to align themselves in a way that created a magnetic force, and the bolt became a magnet.

Caution: *Wires can become hot during this activity.*

Magnet On, Magnet Off

Electromagnets are useful because their magnetism can be turned on and off. In junkyards, electromagnets are used to move old cars around.

Horseshoe Field

Patterns of magnetic fields are revealed when we can see the attraction.

What You'll Need:

horseshoe magnet

paper

iron filings

PLACE A HORSESHOE MAGNET ON A TABLE, and cover it with a sheet of thin paper. Sprinkle iron filings on the paper. Observe the pattern that the iron filings make as they are attracted to the magnet. This pattern gives you an idea of the shape of the field generated by the magnet. The filings show you a two-dimensional version of the field; the real field extends out from the magnet in all directions.

Check around your house to see if you have other magnets, such as round or square ones that might be stuck to your refrigerator. Experiment with these in the same way to see what patterns they make.

Powerful Pole
A horseshoe magnet has lines of force that go from the north pole to the south pole of the magnet. Iron filings sprinkled on paper over a horseshoe magnet reveal these lines of force.

Tennis Cannon

Transferring energy from one object to another can sometimes be a blast.

What You'll Need:

basketball

tennis ball

HOLD A BASKETBALL IN ONE HAND and a tennis ball in the other, and drop them to the ground from the same height. Watch carefully to see how high they bounce. Did one bounce higher than the other? Now hold the basketball in one hand, and place the tennis ball on top of the basketball with your other hand. Drop them to the ground together. Watch carefully to see how high they bounce.

The tennis ball and basketball have energy from falling. The amount of energy depends on the weight of the object. The basketball is much heavier, so it contains much more energy. When the tennis ball and basketball hit the ground, a lot of the energy of the falling basketball is transferred to the tennis ball, and it launches the tennis ball like a cannon.

Two Types of Flies

Momentum depends upon two things: mass and speed. A fly and a baseball may both travel at 15 miles per hour, but the baseball has far more momentum because it has more mass. Which do you think would do more damage to a window, the fly or the baseball?

Heat Sheet

Conductors lead the heat in this activity.

What You'll Need:

paper

scissors

aluminum foil

two thermometers

paper and pen

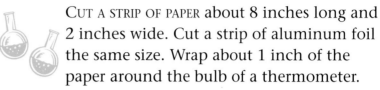

CUT A STRIP OF PAPER about 8 inches long and 2 inches wide. Cut a strip of aluminum foil the same size. Wrap about 1 inch of the paper around the bulb of a thermometer. Wrap about 1 inch of the aluminum foil around the bulb of another thermometer. Find a windowsill that has an area in the shade and an area in the sun. Put the two thermometers on the windowsill so that the thermometers are completely in the shade but the ends of the paper and aluminum foil are in the sun. Record the starting temperatures for both thermometers. Then record the temperatures every few minutes.

The thermometer with the foil heated to a higher temperature because the aluminum is a better conductor of heat. Energy from the sunlight heated the aluminum foil and paper. Aluminum is a good conductor of heat, so it transferred much of the heat to the thermometer. Paper is a poor conductor of heat, so it transferred little of the heat to the thermometer.

Shaken, Not Stirred

Friction is what heats up this experiment.

What You'll Need:

coffee can with lid

sand

thermometer

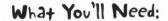

paper and pen

FILL A COFFEE CAN HALFWAY with sand. Measure the temperature of the sand, and write it down. Remove the thermometer, place the lid securely on the can, and shake the can rapidly for a few minutes. Measure the temperature of the sand, and write it down again. Repeat the test one more time.

The energy you used to shake up the can made the sand particles rub against each other and against the side of the can. This created friction, and the friction produced heat. The sand particles acted in a similar way to molecules from two different surfaces that are rubbed against each other.

Essential Oil

Friction can create a lot of heat. Motor oil in cars reduces friction in the engine. If the car loses its oil, there is greater friction, and the car may overheat or even get engine damage.

You Repulse Me

Once you change the charge of these balloons they won't want to be anywhere near each other.

What You'll Need:

balloons

string

tape

cloth (wool, polyester, or nylon)

BLOW UP TWO BALLOONS. Tie strings to each, about 15 inches long. Tape the strings to the edge of a table so the balloons hang down about 1 inch apart from each other. Charge one balloon by rubbing it with a cloth. Then charge the other balloon in the same way. Let both balloons hang near each other, and watch what they do.

Rubbing balloons with the cloth transferred electrons to the balloons. This made both balloons negatively charged. When the balloons were brought near each other, the charge acted to push the balloons away from each other. Objects with the same charge repel each other.

Charge Me Up!

Electrons have a negative charge and form layers (or shells) around the nucleus of an atom. Objects become charged because they gain or lose electrons. A positively charged object lost electrons and a negatively charged object gained electrons.

Light On

Electricity doesn't do much good unless it has a complete circuit.

What You'll Need:

1.5-volt flashlight bulb

electrical wire

D battery

DO YOU THINK YOU CAN CREATE a complete electrical circuit using just a lightbulb, one wire, and one D battery? To make a complete circuit, you have to create a path that allows electrons to flow from the battery to the lightbulb and back to the battery. If you do that, electrical current will flow through your circuit and cause the lightbulb to light. The solution to this problem is to hold a wire on the bottom of the battery, hold the lightbulb on top of the battery, and then connect the wire to the side of the lightbulb. This combination gives a complete circuit for the electricity to flow.

Caution: *Wires can become hot during this activity.*

A Circle of Energy

Electricity needs a complete circuit in order to flow. When electricity flows through a light bulb, electrical energy is converted into heat and light energy.

Light Is Right!

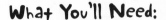

Complete electrical circuits are the key to succeeding at this game.

What You'll Need:

cardboard

brads

marker

electrical wire

1.5-volt lightbulb

9-volt battery

tape

IN THIS PROJECT, you create a quiz card. Think of pairs of items that can be matched. They can be states and their capitals, chemical names and their formulas, and so on. Push six brads into a piece of cardboard in two vertical rows of three each. If you chose states and capitals, make the left row represent the states and the right row represent the capitals. Write the names of the states and capitals on the cardboard next to the brads.

On the back of the cardboard, connect an electrical wire to each brad that represents a state; connect the other end of each wire to the brad that represents that state's capital. Tape a 1.5-volt lightbulb to the back of the card so it sticks above the top of the cardboard, and tape a 9-volt battery to the cardboard just below the bulb. Connect a wire from one terminal of the battery to the bottom of the bulb, and tape it in place. Connect another wire to the side of the base of the bulb. This wire should be long enough so that the other end can reach the front of the cardboard and touch any of the brads on the left; it will be one probe. Connect a wire to the other terminal of the battery. This wire should be long enough so that the other end can reach the front of the cardboard and touch any of the brads on the right; it will be the other probe. Cover the back of the quiz board with another sheet of cardboard.

Now touch the probe for the left side to any of the brads on the left. Choose the matching answer, and touch that brad with the other probe. The light should light, providing positive reinforcement for a correct answer!

Caution: *Wires can become hot during this activity.*

Where's the North Pole?

What direction are you facing right now? You'll know the answer when you make this handy homemade compass.

What You'll Need:

pie pan

water

dishwashing liquid

magnet

needle

¼-inch slice of cork

FILL A PIE PAN WITH WATER. Add a small amount of dishwashing liquid. Now you'll need to magnetize a needle. To do this, use a bar magnet with the north end marked. Scrape the needle across the north end of the magnet, from the eye of the needle to its point. Do this about 15 times. It's important to scrape the needle in the same direction every time—don't rub it back and forth on the magnet.

Carefully poke the needle through a small piece of cork. Float the cork in the middle of the pie pan. Like magic, the needle will always point north. If you walked far enough in that direction, you'd find yourself at the North Pole! That's because the earth is like a giant magnet, with one end in the North Pole and the other end in South Pole.

The Flat Earth

About 2,300 years ago, a Greek philosopher named Aristotle decided that the earth was round, not flat like other people believed. Most people laughed at Aristotle, and it wasn't until Columbus traveled to America in the late 1400s that others started to take Aristotle's theory seriously.

Liquid Melodies

Have you ever noticed all the different sounds that water makes? Learn how to make music with water.

What You'll Need:

bottles, jars, or drinking glasses of different sizes

water

spoon or stick

GO AROUND YOUR HOUSE AND YARD, and see how many different sounds you can make with water. Try the faucets, from barely on to full blast. Listen to the shower, the hose, the sprinkler. Drop ice cubes into a glass of water. Any other ideas? Now think of water sounds in nature: a soft rain, a hard rain, waves, a waterfall. It's a regular symphony, isn't it?

Speaking of a symphony, here's one way to make music with water. Gather several glass bottles, jars, and/or drinking glasses of different shapes and sizes. (Always be careful when handling glass.) Put water in them—a little water or a lot. Use a spoon or a small stick to tap the containers, and see what different notes they make. Can you arrange the containers from lowest note to highest note? Can you change the level of water in the containers to create new notes? How about making up a song to play on your water instruments?

Chapter 7

Beyond Earth

EARTH IS JUST one planet orbiting around one star—the sun. In the vast reaches of space, billions of other stars also shine, and some may have planets that orbit around them too. But as far as we know, Earth is the only planet that supports life.

Ancient people spent a great deal of time studying the stars. They gave names to groups of stars so they could better remember them. Knowing the location of stars helped them as they sailed around the world.

Our solar system contains the sun and nine planets that orbit the sun. These planets, in order from the sun, are Mercury, Venus, Earth, Mars, Jupiter, Saturn, Uranus, Neptune, and Pluto. Some of these planets have

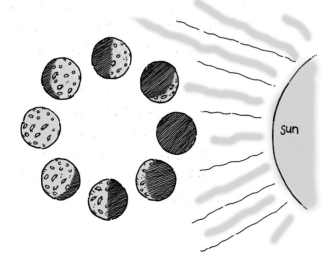

sun

moons that orbit around them. Earth has one moon, which orbits Earth every 27⅓ days.

Feel free to get a little spacey as you work on the projects and activities in this chapter. They're out of this world!

Map of the Stars

Star light, star bright, the first star I see tonight...

What You'll Need:
star chart

THE PATTERNS OF STARS remain the same, but their positions in the sky change. Star charts help us find constellations in the sky. (Star charts are available at bookstores or on the World Wide Web.)

Bring a star chart outside on a clear night. Set the chart to the correct date and time. Hold the chart in front of you as you face north. Look at the chart and sky to see if you can find constellations. Find the Big Dipper and the Little Dipper. At the end of the handle of the Little Dipper is the North Star. Another way to find the North Star is from the Big Dipper. The part of the cup away from the handle is made of two stars. Start from the bottom star, and follow an imaginary line to the upper star. This will point you to the North Star. The North Star is important in navigation because it can always be used to identify which direction is north.

North Star

Little Dipper

To North Star

Big Dipper

Keep On Moving!
Stars seem to move from the east to the west. This is like the sun, our star, which rises in the east and sets in the west. However, the stars aren't moving. The apparent movement of the stars occurs because the earth is rotating.

Head, Ball, Moon

Sometimes we only see a slice of the moon lit up because of our angle of view when we look at it.

What You'll Need:

balls

THE NEXT TIME YOU ARE OUTSIDE and you can see the moon during the day, get a big ball, such as a basketball or a soccer ball. Stand in a sunny spot, face the moon, and hold the ball in front of you as if you were giving it to the moon. Your head, the ball, and the moon should all be lined up. Look at how the sunlight is shining on the ball. Although half of the ball is lit up, you can only see a portion of the lit ball. Now look at the moon. The portion of the ball you see lit up is the same as the portion of the moon that is lit up.

What's a Moonbow?

While most people have seen a rainbow, how many have seen a moonbow? A moonbow occurs when three conditions are met: the moon will be full that night, it has just rained, and the moon has just risen. When all those conditions happen at the same time, a moonbow may appear.

Boxed Moon

Simulate the phases of the moon with this exercise in perception.

What You'll Need:

shoe box

scissors

flashlight

spool of thread

glue

tennis ball

books

CUT A HOLE IN ONE END OF A SHOE BOX big enough for a flashlight to fit through. Then cut eight peep holes around the box as indicated in the drawing. Glue a spool of thread to the center of the bottom of the box. Glue a tennis ball on top of the spool. Prop the flashlight on a stack of books, and shine its light through the hole. Look at the image of the "moon" from the eight different peep holes around the box. What does the moon look like from each peep hole?

As you look at the ball from different angles, different parts of it will appear to be lit up. Our view of the moon changes in the same way. The amount of sunlight hitting the moon does not change throughout the month (unless there is a lunar eclipse, which is rare). Our view of the moon changes because we see it from different angles as it orbits around the earth.

Make a Sundial

Before there were clocks, ancient people used sundials to tell time.

What You'll Need:

thin cardboard

tape

wooden board

pen or marker

CUT A PIECE OF THIN CARDBOARD to the dimensions shown in the illustration. Tape the cardboard upright on a board. Put the sundial outdoors in a sunny place with the highest point of the triangle facing south. Starting as soon as it gets light, go to your sundial every hour on the hour, and mark where the shadow of the cardboard falls. For example, at 7 A.M., write "7 A.M." at the place where the shadow falls. Once all the hours are marked you can use your sundial to tell time. Make sure you place your sundial in exactly the same spot each time you use it.

Can you think of ways that clocks are an improvement over sundials? The most obvious is that clocks tell time at night, too, while sundials don't. What other benefits can you think of?

6" 45° 45° Fold 6"

Shadow marks time

Primitive Clocks

Sundials can help tell time but they don't always work very well. If you traveled north or south from where you took your initial reading, the sundial won't give the correct time. Also, the shapes of the shadows on a sundial change with the seasons.

Sunrise, Sunset

You'll have to wake up early to keep track of where the sun rises.

What You'll Need:

paper and pen

GET UP EARLY ONE MORNING and watch the sun rise. You'll see it best by an open area, such as a beach, lakeshore, or large, flat field. Notice where the sun rises in relation to fixed objects (such as hills or trees) near the horizon. You may want to make notes about this. (For example, you might write: "Sun rose just to the right of the big hill.") Make a diagram showing the eastern and western horizons. Mark where you saw the sun rise. The same day (or as soon as you can), go to the same place and watch the sun set. Again, notice where the sun sets in relation to hills or trees on the horizon. Mark the spot on your diagram.

About three months later, repeat the activity. Notice where the sun rises and sets in relation to those same hills or trees. (Check your notes from last time.) Mark the spots on your diagram. Has the sun moved? The sun always rises in the east and sets in the west. It's really the earth that has moved. As the earth orbits the sun, it changes how much it tilts toward the sun. The result is that the sun rises and sets in different places on the horizon. Always be careful not to look directly at the sun.

Our Sun

There are millions of stars in our galaxy, and the sun is just one of them. The sun, however, is the center of our solar system, and all of the planets in our solar system revolve around the sun. The diameter of the sun is about 865,000 miles, which is more than 100 times that of the earth. More than one million planets the size of the earth would fit into the sun.

Time Flies

Learn about the parts of the moon's cycle with a lunar phases flip book.

What You'll Need:

eight plain white
index cards

black marker

heavy-duty stapler

THE MOON IS ANOTHER GREAT EXAMPLE of nature's cycles. Every 29½ days, the moon goes through a complete cycle. The moon begins the cycle being apparently invisible. This happens when the moon comes between the sun and the earth, so that sunlight only shines on the back side of the moon where we can't see it. As the moon moves around the earth, we see more of the sunlit part of the moon. Halfway through the cycle we see a full moon. At that time, the whole face of the moon is lighted up by the sun. Then we see less and less of the moon until finally it disappears again.

On eight index cards, draw the phases as shown on this page. Draw each "moon" on the right half of the card. Stack the cards in order, with the first one on top of the stack. Staple all the cards together on the left side, or just hold the cards together firmly. With your other hand, flip through the stack to see the moon go through its phases.

Going Through a Phase

Make a model of the sun, earth, and moon to show the phases of the moon.

What You'll Need:

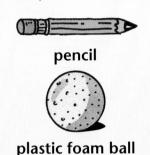

pencil

plastic foam ball

lamp with a
removable shade

STICK A PENCIL into a plastic foam ball. The ball will represent the moon. Use the pencil as a handle.

Darken the room, and then turn on a lamp that doesn't have a shade. Put the lamp at eye level in the middle of the room. Now face the lamp. The lamp is the sun and you are the earth! Hold the plastic foam ball directly between you and the light. The side of the ball that is facing you will be dark. This phase of the moon would be called the "new moon."

Now, hold the ball at arm's length while you turn in place. You might want to hold the ball above your head so the light can always reach it as you turn. Watch the ball. It will go through the phases of the moon as different sides of the ball are exposed to different levels of light. When you are between the lamp and the ball, with the light shining completely on the ball, the ball will be in the phase called the "full moon."

The Moving Moon

One half of the moon is lit up throughout all of the phases of the moon. As the moon rotates, you can see different fractions of the lit portion.

It's Raining Stars

Turn your umbrella into your own private planetarium.

What You'll Need:

black umbrella

white chalk

star chart

DO THIS ACTIVITY on a crystal-clear night when the moon is either invisible or very small. If you can, go to a place where there are few or no human-made lights.

Ask an adult if you can mark up an old, black umbrella with chalk. Open the umbrella and hold it over your head. Point the tip of the umbrella at the North Star. (Use a star chart to find the North Star, or ask an adult to help you.) Look up at the underside of the umbrella. You may see the stars shining through. Use white chalk to mark on the umbrella each place where you see a star. (This will be easier if someone else holds the umbrella for you.) If you can't see the stars through the umbrella, just look in the sky and mark the stars in the same positions as you see them in the sky. When you've marked all the stars you can see, take the umbrella inside. Compare your marks to a star chart. What stars and constellations did you mark? Draw lines connecting the constellations, and label them with their names.

Stargazer

On a clear night, you can probably see only 3,000 stars out of the millions of stars in the sky. Some stars appear much brighter than others. This is because they are either larger, have a stronger light, or are closer to the earth than other stars. The star nearest to the earth, other than our sun, is Proxima Centauri, which is about 25 trillion miles away!

Peas In Space!

Or would you rather have the walnuts?
Make a true scale model of the solar system.

What You'll Need:

a ball that is about 27 inches in diameter (such as a beach ball)

five peas

one orange

one tangerine

two walnuts

tape measure

 YOU'VE PROBABLY SEEN lots of drawings and diagrams of the solar system. But, to make the drawings fit on a piece of paper, the artists have to draw the planets closer together than they really are. In this activity, you'll make a scale model of the solar system. You'll be surprised to see how much bigger some planets are than others, and how far apart some of them are.

Make your model in a large open area that will represent outer space. Put a beach ball or other large ball at one end of

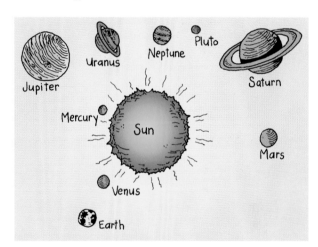

your area. The ball is the sun. Place the other objects as follows. (Remember to measure each planet from the sun.)

Planet	Object	Distance from the Sun
Mercury	Pea	1¾ inches
Venus	Pea	3¼ inches
Earth	Pea	4½ inches
Mars	Pea	7 inches
Jupiter	Orange	2 feet
Saturn	Tangerine	3 feet, 7 inches
Uranus	Walnut	7 feet, 3 inches
Neptune	Walnut	11 feet, 4 inches
Pluto	Pea	14 feet, 10 inches

Chapter 8:

On Earth

ᗷᗷᗷᗷᗷᗷᗷᗷᗷᗷᗷᗷᗷᗷᗷᗷᗷᗷᗷᗷᗷᗷᗷᗷᗷᗷᗷᗷᗷᗷᗷᗷᗷ

Tᴀʟʟ ᴍᴏᴜɴᴛᴀɪɴꜱ, rushing rivers, all kinds of rocks, and wide oceans—these are just some of the nonliving features of the earth. How did it get to look this way? The answer is: S-L-O-W-L-Y. Over millions of years, the earth's surface changed due to volcanic eruptions, earthquakes, erosion, and the movement of glaciers. These activities are still going on today—the earth constantly changes.

Rocks are continually being made and broken down. Rocks are made out of minerals. Some minerals are made of only one element, such as copper or carbon. For example, diamonds are a mineral only made out of carbon molecules. Some minerals are composed of two or more elements. High pressures and temperatures combine the minerals that form rocks. But the weather destroys rocks. For example, water seeps into rocks, freezes, and then breaks the rocks apart into small pieces.

We better keep moving in order to keep up with our changing planet! This chapter's projects will keep you moving and shaking as we learn more about our planet's processes.

The Heat Is On

~~~~~~

Some things are easier to heat than others.

What You'll Need:

two containers

soil

water

two thermometers

tape

lamp

pen and paper

watch or clock

 FILL A CONTAINER halfway with soil. Fill another container one quarter of the way with water. Place a thermometer in each container just underneath the surface of the soil and water, and tape them into position on the sides of the containers. Check the temperature of the soil and of the water. Add more water to the container to make it half full and to make the water temperature the same as the soil temperature. If the water is cooler than the soil, add warm water; if the water is warmer than the soil, add cool water. Put a lamp over the containers so they both get the same amount of light and heat. Record the temperature every 2 minutes. Do this for about 20 minutes.

Your results should have demonstrated that the soil warmed at a faster rate than the water. More energy is needed to raise the temperature of water than of land.

Fan of the Weather

Sometimes the wind can have an effect on the temperature.
Find out why when you try this activity.

What You'll Need:

two thermometers

paper and pen

fan

glass of water

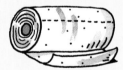

paper towel

READ AND RECORD the temperatures shown on two thermometers. Place one in the breeze of a fan and the other away from the fan. What do you think will happen to the temperature of the thermometer in the breeze? Many people might suspect that this thermometer will cool off and show a lower temperature. But as you will find, this does not occur. The breeze on the thermometer does not lower its temperature.

Allow a small glass of water to warm to room temperature. Wet a paper towel with this water. Place a small wad of the wet paper towel on the bulb of one thermometer. Do nothing to the second thermometer. Place both thermometers in the breeze of the fan. Record the temperatures every couple of minutes.

Was there a difference this time? The temperature of the thermometer with the wet towel on it dropped steadily. The breeze from the fan caused the water to evaporate, and as it evaporated, it used energy in the form of heat. This cooled the thermometer in the same way that your body cools itself when you perspire.

Flushed or Pale?

Body temperature is also regulated by the widening or narrowing of our blood vessels in the skin. When it is hot, and we need to release heat, the blood vessels get wider to increase blood flow, and we look flushed. When it is cold, and we need to conserve heat, the blood vessels narrow, and we look pale.

Sedimental Journey

Witness the way layers of different materials form in water.
This activity will show part of how sedimentary rocks are formed.

What You'll Need:

jar with lid

soil

sand

fine gravel

water

PUT A HANDFUL EACH OF SOIL, sand, and fine gravel into a jar. Fill the jar with water, and screw the lid on tightly. Shake the jar so that all the materials are shaken up. Allow the contents of the jar to settle overnight. Check the jar, and observe the layers that were produced by the different materials.

The soil, sand, and gravel all contained several different materials. The heavier materials sank to the bottom of the jar first. The lighter materials sank last. The different materials formed layers based on their weight. Thus, rocks were at the bottom, and clay particles were at the top. Some organic materials, such as leaves or twigs, might not have sunk at all. When water carries sediments to lakes and oceans, the sediments there form layers in the same way. Over time, pressure can force the particles together so they become sedimentary rocks.

Elementary Science

Just eight simple elements make up 98 percent of the rocks in the world today. What eight elements do you think they might be? If you guessed oxygen, silicon, aluminum, iron, calcium, sodium, potassium, and magnesium, then take a bow—because you're right!

Break Out!

Water has immense power in all of its forms. Take a look at what happens when you freeze an egg to get an idea of what freezing water can do.

What You'll Need:

freezer

egg

bowl

PLACE AN EGG IN A BOWL and put it into the freezer for about five hours. Take it out, and carefully observe how it has changed.

When the materials inside the egg froze, they expanded and broke the hard outer shell of the egg. This process is similar to when water gets into cracks in rocks and freezes. When the water expands, it sometimes breaks the rocks. This is a type of weathering that can make changes in the features of the earth's surface.

The Amazing, Expanding Ice Cube

When things get cold they usually contract (get smaller). Water is an exception to this rule. When water freezes, it gets bigger. The expansion of water when it freezes sometimes breaks up rocks and roads.

Grazing Glaciers

Glaciers are responsible for the way some of the earth's landscape looks today. Build your own glacier in this activity.

What You'll Need:

gravel

paper cup

water

knife

YOU ARE GOING to make a glacier. Put enough gravel in a paper cup to cover the bottom. Fill the cup three quarters of the way with water, and put it in the freezer. When the water is frozen, carefully cut away the bottom inch of paper from the cup. This exposes the ice and gravel but leaves a place for you to hold the ice. Find a patch of soil. Rub the ice and gravel part of your "glacier" over the soil. What effects did this have on the soil? During the last ice age, many places in the north were overrun with glaciers. The movement of these glaciers removed soil and rock and left deep gouges in the earth.

Caution: *This project requires adult supervision.*

Glacial Landscape

Glaciers are huge pieces of ice. Precipitation and cold weather cause the ice to build up and spread. Sometimes a glacier will move and gather rocks and other debris. The glacier pulls the rocks across land, which flattens or scars the surface of the earth.

Making an Impression

*Leave your mark on the world (or at least on plaster)
when you create your own "fossils."*

What You'll Need:

**small natural object
(shell, bone, or leaf)**

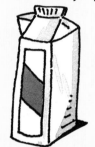

petroleum jelly

plaster of Paris

water

**small disposable dish
(such as a
margarine tub)**

FOSSILS ARE IMPRINTS of plants and animals found in rocks. Here is one way fossils are made in nature: A leaf falls into wet, sandy ground. A flood deposits more sandy soil on top of the leaf, so that it is trapped there. Over thousands of years, the leaf decays and disappears. But as the sandy soil hardens into rock, the impression made by the leaf is left in the rock. You can see how fossils are created by making your own.

First, choose an object to fossilize. It could be a shell, a leaf, an animal bone, or another object from nature. Coat the object with petroleum jelly. Next, pour

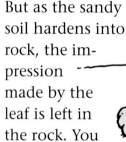

some plaster of Paris and some water in a small dish. Mix them together well. Let the plaster of Paris and water sit for a few minutes without stirring it. Press the object into the plaster of Paris, and let everything dry. This will take at least one day.

When the plaster of Paris is completely dry, remove the object. The impression left behind is like a fossil.

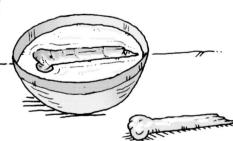

Mineral Testing Kit

Super rock hounds will want to put together this simple kit for identifying minerals and testing their properties.

What You'll Need:

canvas or denim scraps

needle and thread

thick string   penny

small piece of glass

piece of unglazed tile

file or pocket knife

small bottle of vinegar

eyedropper   rocks

reference book about rocks

MAKE A SMALL, sturdy bag to carry your kit: Cut two 6″ × 8″ pieces of canvas or denim and put them together, wrong side out. Sew three sides together. Fold over 1″ of fabric along the opening and stitch all the way around to form a casing. Make a small slit (about ½″) in the casing and slip a drawstring through it.

Into the bag, put a penny, a small piece of glass, a piece of unglazed tile, a file or pocket knife, a bottle of vinegar, and an eyedropper. Use your kit to test and identify rocks and minerals.

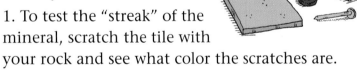

1. To test the "streak" of the mineral, scratch the tile with your rock and see what color the scratches are.

2. Vinegar is used to test for the presence of calcium carbonate. Put a drop of vinegar on the rock. If it fizzes, the rock contains calcium carbonate.

3. The rest of the items test for hardness, on a hardness scale of 1 to 10.

> 1–2: fingernail can scratch rock
>
> 3: penny can scratch rock
>
> 4–5: knife blade or file can scratch rock
>
> 6: glass can scratch rock
>
> 7: rock can scratch knife or file; rock can barely scratch glass
>
> 8–10: harder than common minerals

Use what you learn to try to identify the rocks that you have been testing in a reference book about rocks.

Be a Mineral Detective

Calcium carbonate is one of the most common minerals in nature. See if you can discover some in your home.

What You'll Need:

wide-mouthed jar

vinegar

raw egg (in the shell)

different kinds of chalk

BOTH EGGSHELLS AND LIMESTONE contain calcium carbonate, and some chalk is made from it. It's simple to find out whether or not a substance has calcium carbonate in it. Simply drop a sample into a jar that has some vinegar in it. If the vinegar dissolves (or partly dissolves) the substance, it contains calcium carbonate.

To try this, fill a wide-mouthed jar with vinegar. Gently place a whole egg in the jar. Watch the eggshell begin to fizz. Over a couple of days, it will completely dissolve! That's because an eggshell is almost all calcium carbonate.

Try the same thing with several different chalk samples. If the chalk is made from calcium carbonate, it will fizz and at least partly dissolve. Some chalk is made from another mineral called gypsum, which will not fizz or dissolve in vinegar.

Brushing Your Teeth With Rocks

Calcium carbonate is found in rocks such as limestone and marble. It is used to make toothpaste, cleaning powders, and white paint.

Washed Away

Learn how erosion—when soil is washed away by wind or water—occurs.

What You'll Need:

three aluminum-foil cooking pans

three lengths of rubber or plastic tubing (½-inch in diameter)

tape

a mixture of soil, sand, and clay

potting soil

books

three bowls   **cereal grains**

POKE A SMALL HOLE in one end of each pan, near the upper rim. Put one end of a length of tubing into each hole, using tape to hold it there. Into each pan put a layer of the soil, sand, and clay mixture. Then add a layer of potting soil on top of that. Put all three pans indoors in a place where they will get sunlight. Rest all three pans on books to elevate the pans at about a 30-degree angle. The tubing should be on the bottom end of each pan. Put the free end of each tube into a bowl.

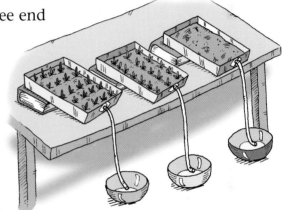

In one pan, make rows across the width of the pan and plant cereal grains in the rows. In another pan, make the rows lengthwise and plant the grain. Don't plant anything in the third pan. Use a plant mister to keep the grain moist until it sprouts. Continue to water the grain until the seedlings are about two inches tall. Don't do anything to the empty pan. Once the seedlings in the two pans are about two inches tall, begin using a watering can to sprinkle all three pans. The watering can should have a spout that sprinkles, imitating rain. Each time you water the pans, watch the water that runs into the bowls. Which bowl collects more potting soil? Why? What could you do to prevent potting soil from eroding into the bowls?

That Settles It!

When soil, sand, and other materials settle at the bottom of a lake or pond, it is called sediment. Over time, layers of sediment can form rock.

What You'll Need:

jar with lid

soil

sand

gravel

water

small, plastic animals

PUT A HANDFUL each of soil, sand, and gravel into a jar. Add a few small, plastic animals to the jar. Fill the jar with water. Put the lid on tightly. Shake the jar well until everything is mixed together. Now let the jar sit overnight. In the morning, see how the different things in the jar have settled.

This experiment shows how fossilized critters are sometimes made. How would you describe what you see? What can you say about the layers? Compare your layers to what happens in a lake or pond.

A Timely Procedure

Sedimentary rock is made of sediment (which can be all kinds of small particles). The layers of sediment settle and form over thousands of years. Over time, pressure converts these layers into hard rock.

Chapter 9:
Weather

W E EXPERIENCE the weather every day. It is something that we often think about and talk about. Weather occurs in the lower part of the earth's atmosphere (called the "troposphere"). Air temperature, humidity, and the wind's speed and direction are important parts of the weather.

Temperature measures how hot or cold it is. On a hot day, you sweat and it evaporates from your skin. This cools your body down. If a warm day is humid (there is a lot of water vapor in the air), you feel warmer. This is because the sweat cannot evaporate as easily from your skin. Cold days can feel even colder if it is windy. The wind blows heat away from our bodies. Precipitation—rain, sleet, and hail—is another part of weather.

The day-to-day influence of weather creates the different climates on the earth. Climate has a big impact on our lives. It influences the crops we can grow, how we dress, and perhaps even how we feel. Climate influences almost all aspects of life. For example, if an area has very warm temperatures and lots of rain, it might become a tropical rain forest. Another area with high temperatures and very little rain might be a desert.

The weather may be unpredictable, but you can count on the activities in this chapter to help you understand our planet's climate a little better.

The Dew Point

It is easy to study water in all of its forms. Here we will take a look at the relationship between temperature and water vapor.

What You'll Need:

metal can
with no label

warm water

food coloring

ice cubes

spoon

FILL A CLEAN METAL CAN about two thirds of the way with warm water, and add a few drops of food coloring. Let the can sit on a table for one hour until it reaches room temperature. Add ice cubes to the water one at a time, and stir with a spoon. Watch the outside of the can. After you add enough ice cubes, the outside of the can will become wet with small droplets of clear water. Notice that the drops on the outside are clear and that the water inside the can is colored; the drops did not come from the water inside the can.

The air outside the can contains water vapor. When the vapor in the air came in contact with the cold can, the vapor's temperature lowered, and it condensed into liquid water on the outside of the can.

Making a Barometer

Barometers measure air pressure. They are used to help people predict the weather. Make your own barometer and keep your eyes on the sky!

What You'll Need:

modeling clay

two rulers

water

large bowl

narrow, clear plastic bottle

string

pen and paper

tape

STICK THE END OF A RULER into a ball of modeling clay. Flatten the bottom of the clay so that it will hold the ruler upright on a table. Pour about 3 inches of water into a large bowl. Fill a narrow, clear plastic bottle three-quarters of the way with water. Cover the opening of the bottle with your hand, turn the bottle upside down, and carefully lower the neck of the bottle into the bowl. When the opening of the bottle is beneath the water, remove your hand from the opening. Put the ruler on its clay stand into the bowl of water, and stand it right next to the bottle. Use two pieces of string to attach the bottle to the ruler so that the bottle will stand upright.

Take a piece of paper about 1″ wide and 4″ long, and put a mark every ¼″ on the long side of the paper. Tape this paper scale on the plastic bottle so that about one-third of the paper scale is above the water line in the bottle. Observe your barometer each morning and evening. You will see that the level of the water in the bottle changes from day to day.

If air pressure rises, the air will press down more on the surface of the water in the bowl and raise the level in the bottle. If the air pressure falls, the air will press down less on the water in the bowl and lower the level in the bottle. A drop in air pressure usually signifies bad weather approaching (and vice versa). Use your barometer to predict weather changes. Keep track of your predictions to see how well you do.

Clock the Wind

How fast is the wind blowing today?
Make a wind-speed gauge that will tell you.

What You'll Need:

two hollow balls (rubber, tennis, or ping-pong balls)

knife

nails

1′ wooden 2×4, a board for a base, and two sticks of the same length

drill

wax or oil

ASK AN ADULT to help you with this project. First, take two small, hollow balls and cut them in half. Nail the ball halves to the ends of two sticks with the cut sides facing outward, as shown in the illustration. Paint one ball half a different color from the other three. Next, nail the two sticks together at right angles so they form an X. Make sure you join the two sticks at their exact centers, so the joined sticks will balance on the nail. Use a long nail so that the end of the nail comes through both sticks.

Now make the base. Have an adult drill a hole in the end of a 1′ length of a wooden 2×4. The hole should be a bit larger than the nail that holds the two sticks together. Attach the 2×4 to a wooden base, and set the nail in the drilled hole. (Put a little wax or oil in the hole so the gauge will turn easily.)

Now, put your wind-speed gauge in the wind. Count the number of times it turns around in 30 seconds. (Count by the painted ball half.) Write that number down and divide it by five. The answer is the wind speed in miles per hour.

What Kind of Wind?

Be a wind detective! There are clues all around you that help tell how fast the wind is blowing.

IN 1805, Commander Francis Beaufort of the British Navy came up with a system so that sailors had a way to describe the wind's strength that meant the same thing to everybody. The Beaufort scale, listed below, shows how each level of wind looks both at sea and on land. Each day, look for clues to how strong the wind is. Is it a 0 day or a 7 day? Is it a light breeze or a fresh breeze?

The Beaufort Scale

Type of wind	Clues at sea	Clues on land
0 Calm	Smooth water	Smoke rises straight up
1 Light air	Small ripples	Smoke drifts sideways
2 Light breeze	Waves 0–1 feet	Leaves and weather vanes move
3 Gentle breeze	Waves 1–2 feet; foam	Twigs move
4 Moderate breeze	Waves 2–4 feet	Branches move; flags flap
5 Fresh breeze	Waves 4–8 feet; spray	Small trees sway
6 Strong breeze	Waves 8–13 feet	Large branches sway
7 Strong wind	Waves 13–20 feet	Larger trees sway; flags stand straight out
8 Fresh gale	Waves 13–20 feet	Twigs break; hard to walk
9 Strong gale	Waves 13–20 feet	Signs blow down
10 Storm	Waves 20–30 feet	Trees fall over
11 Violent storm	Waves 30–45 feet, foam covers surface	Widespread damage
12 Hurricane	Waves over 45 feet, heavy spray and foam	Widespread destruction

Blowing in the Wind

The wind is sometimes like a bus or train. It picks up passengers from one place and transports them to another.

What You'll Need:

cardboard

string

vegetable oil or petroleum jelly

GET A PIECE OF CARDBOARD that is the size of a piece of notebook paper or larger. Make a small hole on one end of the cardboard, and tie a piece of string through the hole. Smear one side of the cardboard with vegetable oil or petroleum jelly. On a windy day, hang the cardboard from a tree using the string. Make sure the oily side of the cardboard is facing the wind. Leave the cardboard in the wind for an hour or more. Then go back and see what the wind has carried onto the cardboard. You may find seeds, insects, pollen, dust, or other tidbits of nature.

Some plants (such as dandelions) use wind to help scatter their seeds far away. Sometimes the seeds can be carried for several miles or more! Small spiders can hang by their thread and let the wind blow them from spot to spot. What other ways can you think of to use wind?

Trade Winds

Have you ever heard the expression "trade winds"? Long ago, people delivered things that were for sale by ship. Buying and selling items was also known as "trade." Sailors knew about the steady bands of wind that blow all around the world, just above and below the equator. They called these winds the trade winds and used them to travel the world.

Twister in a Bottle

Most real tornadoes are made of air, but you can demonstrate how tornadoes work using water.

What You'll Need:

water

two 2-liter bottles

cardboard

knife

tape

POUR WATER INTO A 2-liter plastic bottle until it is about three-quarters full. Cut a circle of cardboard as big around as the bottle's opening. Then cut a ¼″ hole in the center. Place the cardboard circle on top of your water bottle's opening. Turn another 2-liter bottle upside down and tape the two bottles together, top to top. Wrap the bottle necks with tape, so the connection doesn't leak. Now turn the bottles upside down, so the full bottle is on top. With one hand, hold the bottom bottle to steady it. With the other hand, begin moving the top bottle in a circle. Watch what happens: a tornado in a bottle.

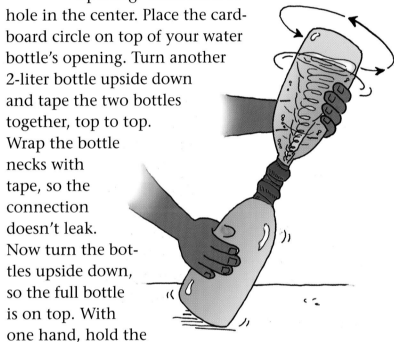

Water tornadoes, such as the one you just made, happen in nature, too. When a tornado forms over water, it's called a waterspout.

Wind Sock

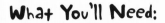

Socks do more than keep your toes warm. A wind sock can tell you which way the wind is blowing—and how fast, too!

What You'll Need:

yardstick

light cloth such as muslin (1 yard will make a large sock)

scissors

needle and thread

wire   **fishing line**

thin wood

stake or old broom handle

large nail

WITH HELP FROM A PARENT or adult, use a yardstick to cut one square yard of light fabric. Fold it in half diagonally. Mark the center of one of the narrow edges. Cut from the mark to the corner at the other end. You will have two long triangles of fabric. Cut 2″ off the pointed end. Sew the long edges together to make a cone. (An adult may be able to help you sew with a sewing machine.) Shape light, stiff wire into a hoop large enough to keep the large end of the cone open. Fold the edges of the fabric around the wire and sew in place. Cut four pieces of heavy fishing line, about 2′ long. Poke four small holes through the fabric around the hoop at even distances. Tie a piece of fishing line through each. Cut a square of wood, and paint letters for each of the four directions on the corners. Glue the square to the top of the stake or old broom handle. Drive a nail through the center of the square. Tie the lines of your wind sock to the nail.

Hang your wind sock outside your home, making sure the letters are facing the correct direction, and observe the angles of the windsock on different days. Note which angles go with what weather conditions. Make a chart of your information and use the chart to help you estimate wind speed.

Weather Vane

*Which way is the wind blowing? With a little work
you'll have your own weather vane to tell you.*

What You'll Need:

18″ strip of wood (about ¼″ thick and ½″ wide), a flat piece of very thin wood (about 4″ long and 3″ wide), and a 4″ square of thin wood

sandpaper

drill   compass

thin wire nails

hot glue gun and glue sticks

small fishing weights

spray paint

small metal nut

one fourpenny nail

stake

WITH ADULT HELP, sand the wood strip smooth. Lay it flat, and drill a small hole 8″ from one end (big enough for the fourpenny nail to go through). Next, cut a fin from thin wood. It should be 4″ long, 3″ wide at one end, and 1″ wide at the other.

Now turn your thin stick so the narrow side faces up. Lay the fin on the narrow side on the end of the stick that is 8″ from the hole. Carefully nail it in place with thin wire nails. Run the fourpenny nail through the hole in the stick. See if the vane balances. If it does not, hot glue small fishing weights opposite the fin. Paint with spray paint. Cut a 4″ square of thin wood and spray paint it. When dry, paint on the letters of the four directions on each of the sides. Paint the stake. When it is dry, glue the painted square of wood to the top. Lay a small nut on the center of the square, then the pointer. Pound the fourpenny nail through the hole in the pointer so that it goes through the nut, the center of the square, and into the stake. Set the weather vane out in an open area. Use a compass to align it. When reading the weather vane, remember that it will point into the wind, showing where the wind is coming from.

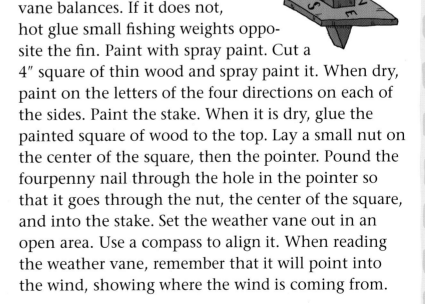

Rain Gauge

Next time it rains, keep track of just how wet it is out there with your own working rain gauge.

What You'll Need:

piece of thin wood (about 8″ long and 4″ wide)

sandpaper

spray paint (optional)

old test tube or olive jar

modeling clay (optional)

wire   drill

6″ plastic ruler

acrylic paint

stake

paper

pen

WITH HELP FROM A PARENT or other adult, sand the piece of wood smooth. If you wish, you can paint it with spray paint. If you are using an old test tube, press a small amount of modeling clay in the bottom to make it level. Next, lay your test tube or olive jar on the board and mark the board so that the top of the jar or tube extends about 1″ beyond the top edge of the board. Mark the board on both sides of the tube near the top and near the bottom. Have an adult drill small holes where you made marks. Wire the tube or olive jar to the board by running wire through the small holes and around the tube. Twist tightly in the back.

Use a ruler to help you paint marks on the side of the tube. Start from the bottom and paint heavy lines every inch. Then paint thin lines to mark quarter inches. Fasten your rain gauge to a stake. Be sure to put it someplace where overhanging trees or large buildings won't block the rain. After a rain, check the tube to see how much rain fell. Then empty the gauge, and return it to the stake. Keep track of your readings on a chart.

Natural Math

You don't have to be a weather forecaster to calculate how far away lightning is. Just take a look.

What You'll Need:

stopwatch or watch with a second hand

WHERE THERE IS LIGHTNING, there is thunder. Since light travels faster than the speed of sound, you see the flash before you hear the crack. You can use the thunder to figure out how far away the lightning is. Watch for a flash of lightning. When you see it, use a stopwatch or second hand to count the seconds between the flash and the thunder that follows it. Write down the number of seconds, and divide that number by five. The answer tells you how far away from you the lightning was in miles.

Did you know that not all lightning bolts touch the earth? In fact, two-thirds of all lightning occurs between clouds or within the same cloud. But that doesn't mean it's safe to go out in a thunderstorm! During a storm, avoid tall objects (like trees), and don't touch anything metal. You should also stay away from electrical appliances, telephones, and water until the storm is over.

Make a Hygrometer

Sometimes people say, "It's not the heat, it's the humidity," to explain why hot weather bothers them. Use this instrument to measure the humidity.

What You'll Need:

one hair at least 9" long

half-gallon cardboard milk carton

scissors

darning needle

broom straw   glue

paper clip   tape

penny

plain index card

WASH THE HAIR CLEAN with soap and water. Under adult supervision, cut a small "H" in the side of the carton as shown, about one-half the length of the darning needle. Bend back the tabs and push the needle through. Poke a broom straw into the eye of the needle and glue in place. At the end of the carton, cut a small slit and push the paper clip through it. Glue it in place. Tape one end of the hair to the paper clip. Lay the hair over the needle, loop it around the needle once, then let it hang over the end of the box opposite the paper clip. Tape the penny to the free end of the hair. Draw a half-circle on the index card, and divide the half-circle with ten marks. Label them one through ten beginning on the left side. Glue the index card to the box under the broom straw. Take your completed hygrometer into the bathroom and run hot water in the shower until the mirror fogs up. The air is 100 percent humid and will cause the hair to stretch. Adjust the straw so it points to 10. Put the hygrometer outdoors in a sheltered place, such as under a porch. Tap it gently a few times before taking a reading, to make sure the straw isn't stuck in place.

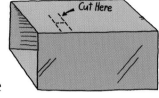

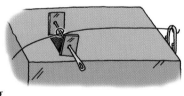

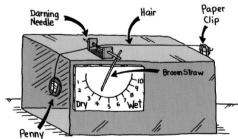

Just How Hot Is It?

Most thermometers are made with mercury, a poisonous metal.
But you can make a safe thermometer using water.

What You'll Need:

soft drink bottle

water

food coloring

clear drinking straw

modeling clay

index card

tape

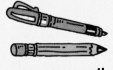

pen or pencil

FILL A SMALL SOFT DRINK BOTTLE almost full of water (about ⅘ full). Color the water with food coloring. Put a clear drinking straw in the bottle so that the straw goes halfway down into the bottle. Use modeling clay to seal the top of the bottle and hold the straw in place. Tape an index card to the straw. You will use the card as a scale. Make a mark on the card to show where the water level is.

Now move your thermometer to a sunny place. Does the water rise? Mark the index card to show the new water level. (You may want to mark it with an "S" for sunny so you'll know which mark is which.) Check your thermometer at different times of the day to see how the temperature varies. You can also compare it with the weather section of your local newspaper to see if your readings are close to the "official" temperature. Write the actual recorded temperature next to each mark you made on your card to see how close your thermometer was.

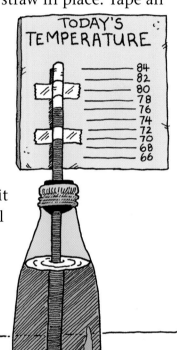

Cricket Degrees

Did you know that crickets are nature's thermometers?
Find out how to tell the temperature by cricket chirps.

What You'll Need:

paper and pen

GO OUT IN THE EVENING to a place where you know there are crickets. Single out the chirp of one cricket, and count its chirps for 14 seconds. Write down the number, and add 40 to it. The sum will tell you the temperature in degrees Fahrenheit.

Crickets make their chirping sounds by rubbing their wings together. Only male crickets chirp, and they only do so when they feel safe and warm. Make sure you are quiet and still while you wait for the crickets to create their song.

Fair Weather Friends
The activity of many insects and reptiles is slow in cold weather and speedy when it is warm.

Rainbow-making

Why wait for rainbows when you can make them yourself?
Here are three ways to add some color to your life.

What You'll Need:

garden hose

prism or hanging crystal ornament

a sheet of white paper

glass pan

water

metal or plastic mirror

RAINBOWS ARE CAUSED BY SUNLIGHT passing through droplets of water in the sky. Water acts just as a prism does, breaking sunlight into its many colors.

The easiest way to make rainbows is to use a garden hose with a spray attachment. On a sunny day, turn on the hose and set the sprayer to make a fine mist. Turn the hose until you can see rainbows in the mist. You might even see a double rainbow. Notice that the order of colors in the second rainbow is reversed.

If you have a prism or a crystal ornament (such as the crystals that dangle from chandeliers), you can make rainbows by holding your prism or crystal in a beam of sunlight. Turn the prism so that the rainbow falls on a white wall, or on a sheet of white paper.

The third way to make rainbows is with a metal or plastic mirror and a wide pan of water. Submerge the mirror in the water and turn it so that sunlight reflects off it and shines on the wall. You can put up white paper to see the rainbows better. You will get wavy, ripply rainbows.

Rainbow Timing

When the sun is low in the sky (around sunrise or sunset), rainbows are larger, and appear as a semicircle (that means half of a circle). Rainbows are more commonly seen at these times of day.

Identifying Clouds

All clouds are made of tiny droplets of water. Yet clouds come in all shapes and sizes, and bring different kinds of weather.

What You'll Need:

paper and pen

THE MAIN KINDS OF clouds are shown below. They're listed from the lowest to the highest in the sky. What type of clouds are in the sky right now? Keep a record of the clouds you see each day. You can draw the clouds and keep a count of how many days you see each type of cloud. Maybe you'll be able to see them all!

Low clouds (up to 6,500 feet)

Fog: Clouds in contact with the ground.
Stratus: Low sheets of clouds that form less than a mile above the earth. Like a thick blanket over the earth, they bring dark, gray days—and, sometimes, drizzle.
Nimbostratus: A thick, dark layer of clouds that brings rain. (Nimbus is Latin for rain.)
Cumulus: These are the big, white fluffy clouds that float by on sunny days. They usually mean good weather.
Stratocumulus: Cumulus clouds pressed together in layers.
Cumulonimbus: These clouds pile up into towering mountains called "thunderheads." They may bring thunderstorms. At their worst, they create tornadoes.

Middle clouds (6,500 to 20,000 feet)

Altocumulus: These are rows of clouds shaped like long rolls.
Altostratus: Thin, gray, layered clouds that look like a veil in front of the sun.

High clouds (20,000 to 40,000 feet)

Cirrus: These long, wispy clouds are often called "mare's tails." Can you guess why?
Cirrocumulus: These rows of long, thin clouds are sometimes called "mackerel sky" because they resemble fish scales or ripples in water.
Cirrostratus: These form thin layers of high clouds that often cause a halo around the sun or moon.

Chapter 10: Keeping a Livable Earth

I F YOU HAVE READ the other chapters in this book and done some of the projects, then you realize that we live on a beautiful and interesting planet. This is our home, and it should be shared among all living things. We rely on other things to give us oxygen and food. Unfortunately, the actions of humans are harming parts of the earth. For instance, pollution affects plant and animal life. Acid rain, brought about by pollution, is responsible for the destruction of a lot of trees in our forests.

The earth can be viewed as a giant terrarium. It has a delicate balance of life. The destruction of trees destroys the sources of food and shelter for other organisms. Then, the loss of those organisms could lead to the extinction of other living things.

Since the actions of people are threatening the earth's balance of nature, we need to actively work to reduce the problems we are causing. For example, when scientists realized that chlorofluorocarbons (or CFCs) in refrigerators and aerosol cans were damaging the earth's ozone layer, governments around the world banned their use.

In this chapter you will build your own terrarium, learn the effects of acid rain, and see how nature recycles. These projects will help you understand more about the importance of not destroying our precious and beautiful planet earth.

Acid Rain Is a Pain

Acid rain is precipitation that is tainted with pollution. It can cause damage to a lot of things on earth, including plants.

What You'll Need:

three potted plants of equal size

three spray bottles

paper and pen

tape

water

vinegar

ruler

FIND A PLACE where you can grow three potted plants for several weeks; make sure the plants will all experience the same growing conditions—sunlight, temperature, and so on. Label the plants and three spray bottles "REGULAR RAIN," "ACID RAIN," and "EXTREME ACID RAIN." Fill the regular rain bottle with tap water. Fill the acid rain bottle two thirds of the way with tap water and one-third of the way with vinegar. Fill the extreme acid rain bottle one-third of the way with tap water and two-thirds of the way with vinegar. Measure and record the heights of the plants. Water each plant with the type of rain indicated on its label. Every week, measure the growth of the three plants. After a few weeks, compare the effects that the different types of rain had on the plants.

Warm Planet, Cold Planet

The earth's atmosphere helps keep our planet warm. This experiment will show you how.

What You'll Need:

two thermometers

two identical jars

clear plastic wrap

paper and pen

PUT A THERMOMETER into each of two identical jars. Cover one jar with plastic wrap, and leave the other one uncovered. Record the temperatures in both jars. Place both jars next to each other on a sunny windowsill for about 20 minutes. Check and record the temperatures of the jars every few minutes. Compare how quickly the temperatures of the two jars rise. Take the jars off the windowsill, and put them somewhere out of the sun for about 20 minutes. Read and record the temperatures of the jars again every few minutes. Compare how quickly the temperatures of the two jars fall.

The jar with the plastic wrap warmed faster and to a higher temperature than the jar without the plastic wrap. The plastic wrap let in the light, and it helped keep the heat inside. The other jar had no covering to hold in the heat. When you took the jars out of the sun, the one with the plastic wrap stayed warmer longer, again because the plastic wrap helped to keep in some of the heat. The gases in the earth's atmosphere act in a similar way. They let sunlight in and help the earth keep some of the heat. A planet without an atmosphere is usually cold because it loses heat quickly, just like the jar without the plastic wrap.

Flash Sun

∿∿∿∿∿∿∿∿∿∿∿∿∿∿∿∿∿∿∿∿∿∿∿∿∿∿∿∿∿∿∿∿∿∿∿∿∿∿∿

Learn how the earth's tilt helps to create the difference in the seasons.

What You'll Need:

two similar flashlights

MANY PEOPLE THINK IT IS COLD in the winter because the earth is farther from the sun during the winter season. This is not true. In fact, in the Northern Hemisphere, the sun is slightly closer to the earth during the winter.

It is colder in the winter because the earth tilts away from the sun and the sun's intensity on the Northern Hemisphere decreases.

To picture this, take two flashlights. Stand close to a wall. Shine one light straight at the wall. Notice the round circle of light it makes. Point the other flashlight slightly upward, and shine it against the wall. Notice the larger oval area of light it makes. Both flashlights put off the same light and heat, but the first one concentrates it in a smaller area, and the other one spreads the light and heat over a greater area. The angled beam is like the sunlight the earth receives in winter and the straight beam is like the sunlight we receive in summer.

Our Sun

There are millions of stars in our galaxy, and the sun is just one of them. The sun, however, is the center of our solar system, and all of the planets in our solar system revolve around the sun. The diameter of the sun is about 865,000 miles, which is more than 100 times that of the earth. More than one million planets the size of the earth would fit into the sun.

Mini-ecosystems

For a science project—or just for fun—make a display of the world's forests, deserts, and grasslands.

What You'll Need:

aquarium or
gallon glass jar

potting soil

sand

charcoal for
houseplants

purchased or
collected plants

"BIOMES" ARE LARGE AREAS of the earth that are determined by the plant communities that grow there. Although some types of plants will grow in a variety of locations and climates, others need specific temperatures, relative humidity, and soil type in order to thrive.

You can re-create the six major biomes of the earth in miniature using terrariums. Clean and dry an aquarium or gallon jar. Pour a ½-inch layer of charcoal in the bottom, then add about four inches of potting soil. (For a desert, use a mixture of equal parts potting soil and sand.) Purchase the types of plants (listed on page 146) for the biome you are creating, or ask someone for permission to collect plants from their property or garden. Never collect plants from State or National Parks or Forests. Doing so is against the law and the plants could be endangered (and therefore, protected). Here is a list of biomes and some suggestions of plants you can use:

Tundra (areas such as Northern Canada and Alaska): lichens, mosses, and any of the small alpine plants sold for rock gardens (such as mountain phlox). These plants will need to be placed by a sunny window.

Northern coniferous forest (areas such as Southern Canada and Northern United States): piggyback plants (also known as thousand-mothers plants) and small ferns will work well. These plants will do well in moderate light (not too much and not too little).

Deciduous forest (areas such as Eastern United States): violets, wintergreens, strawberries, and small ferns. These plants will grow well in partial to full sunlight.

Grassland (areas such as Midwestern United States): Plant a prairie wildflower seed mix that includes some types of grasses. Place your terrarium by a sunny window.

Desert (such as Southwestern United States): cacti and aloe vera plants. Make sure you don't water these plants much. Let soil get very dry between waterings.

Tropical rain forest (such as the Amazon Basin in South America): Most common houseplants come from the tropics. Try African violets, creeping Charlies, or aluminum plants.

Short but Sweet

The arctic region (tundra), in Northern Canada and Alaska, is very cold and dark through much of the year. The climate does warm up, though, for a few months. During those months, the sun shines almost all the time! Over 1,000 species of plants thrive in the tundra. And, although they only bloom for a short period, some of these alpine tundra flowers are much larger and more beautiful than their cousins that live in warmer regions of the planet.

"Don't Go!"

Endangered animals are animals that are in danger of becoming extinct. Find out how to help these vanishing creatures.

What You'll Need:

reference books

poster board

markers

THERE ARE MORE THAN 700 species of animals on the endangered list, including the giant panda, the blue whale, and the bald eagle. Do research to find out some of the other animals that are facing extinction. (Local nature organizations or local zoos are good places to ask.) Then, choose one endangered animal that you especially care about. Learn as much as you can about that animal. Find out where it lives, why it is endangered, and what people are doing to help (and maybe to harm!) it. Most important, find out what you can do to help.

Here's one thing you can do: Make a poster telling others about the animal and how they can help. Try to display your poster in a public place—such as a library or store—where lots of people will see it.

Saving the Animals

An endangered species of animal is one that is in danger of dying out. This danger could be because hunters kill off the animals, or it could be because the animal's environment has changed. People can help reverse the situation, though. In 1965, only 6,000 vicunas—a camel-like animal that lives in South America—were still alive. People killed vicunas for their wool. By protecting the vicuna from hunting, and by giving them an appropriate place to live, there are now more than 160,000 vicunas alive today.

Don't Throw It Away!

If you and your family aren't recycling yet, now is the time to start! Set up your own recycling center.

What You'll Need:

cardboard boxes

marker

RECYCLING IS A GOOD WAY TO HELP nature—and other people. Recycling saves trees, energy, and many other resources that we all need. And recycling helps reduce the amount of pollution and trash in the world.

To start your own recycling center, find out what items can be recycled in your area. (Call city hall or your local newspaper.) Then find out where items to be recycled can be dropped off—or if they can be picked up at your home. It's easy to set up a center at your home so everybody will remember to recycle. Simply put cardboard boxes next to the trash can, and label them: "Newspaper," "Aluminum," and "Glass." These are the items that are most commonly recyclable. In some areas, you can also recycle some kinds of plastic and other kinds of paper (such as magazines and cardboard).

Recycling Facts

While the problem of pollution can seem overwhelming, there are solutions. Paper can be recycled after the ink is removed by a special process, and steel and aluminum cans can be melted down to make new cans. When making glass items, old glass can be added to new glass. This mixture needs a lower temperature during creation, so less energy is needed.

What's It Good For?

Everybody knows that recycling is one good way to help nature. But there's another way, too: Reuse.

What You'll Need:

plastic milk jug

scissors

"RECYCLING" MEANS SAVING THINGS so they can be turned into new products. "Reusing" means using products in new ways, instead of throwing them away. For instance, a plastic milk jug is a product that can be reused in many ways. Here are some ideas:

• Make a watering can for flowers. All you need to do is have an adult cut off the top of the jug, above the handle.

• Plastic milk jugs with the tops cut off make great organizers for craft supplies. Use them to store your nature finds until you're ready to use them.

• Milk jugs are also good containers for sprouting seeds. Have an adult cut the top off to make a flower pot. Then poke holes in the bottom for drainage. You can get your summer vegetables or flowers started inside and transplant them outdoors when the weather gets warmer.

• Make a "drinking fountain" for small wild animals by cutting the jug to make a shallow tray.

Can you think of other products that you could reuse, instead of throwing them away? Each time you go to throw away a package or other product, ask yourself, "How could I use this again?"

Making Paper

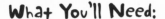

*Recycle your old paper and make new,
unique paper that you can't buy in any store!*

What You'll Need:

stiff wire screen

old paper

bowl

water

blender

iron

RECYCLING PAPER AT HOME is fun and easy, but it can be a little messy! Do this project in the kitchen, and make sure that you have some towels ready for clean-up.

1. With the help of an adult, bend the sharp edges of the wire screen over and flatten them (so nobody will accidentally rub against it and get a cut). You can also make a wooden frame and then staple the wire screen onto it.

2. Tear white scrap paper into small pieces. Then place the torn paper into a bowl of warm water and soak for 15 minutes.

3. Put the soaked paper (which is now called pulp) in the blender with equal amounts of water and blend the mixture until it is mushy. Do not fill the blender more than half-full. If you have a lot of pulp, blend it in batches.

4. Pour the blended pulp into the dish pan or roasting pan. Add a gallon of warm tap water. You should now have a thin slurry (which means a watery mixture) of paper pulp.

5. Tilt the screen away from you, and dip it into the pan with a smooth motion. Hold the screen level under the water, then lift it out of the pan slowly and smoothly. There should be an even layer of pulp sitting on the screen. Tilt the screen slightly to let excess water run off.

6. Set the screen in a safe place to let the pulp dry for a little while (about 30 minutes).

7. Lay a soft, absorbent towel or rag flat out on a table and quickly flip the screen over onto it—pulp side down. Do this step in one quick motion so the dried

**dish pan or
roaster pan**

**rags or tea towels
(use smooth cloth,
not terry cloth)**

pulp doesn't have a chance to slide off. Blot the back of the screen with another rag to absorb any excess water. Gently peel the screen from the sheet. This process of blotting and removing the fresh (recycled) sheet of paper is called "couching" (pronounced "cooching").

8. Let the paper air-dry, or place another cloth over it and have an adult iron it dry and flat. Peel it away while still damp so it doesn't stick to the cloth. Save the leftover pulp by freezing it, or throw it away, but never pour it down the sink or flush it down the toilet!

Check Those Labels!

A lot of companies will let you know if their products are made from recycled materials. Sometimes, this information will be printed somewhere noticeable on the label. Other times, it will be printed by the company information and computer bar code. Always try to buy products that use recycled materials (and encourage your mom or dad to do the same). And, if a product that you like to buy doesn't use recycled materials, write a letter to the company's address listed (or make a phone call if a toll-free number is listed) on the label and ask them why they don't use recycled products. Recycling helps reduce the amount of waste and pollution in the world.

Nature's Recycler

Mother Nature recycles everything. Nature will even help you recycle your garbage, turning it into fertilizer called "compost."

What You'll Need:

plastic garbage can

heavy-duty scissors or shears

dry leaves, grass clippings, or straw

vegetable matter

rake

plant mister

TO MAKE your own composter, cut some holes in a garbage can. Put the garbage can outdoors in a place where animals won't get into it. Put in a layer of dry leaves, grass clippings, and/or straw. On top of that dry layer, you can start adding food scraps. Vegetable and fruit scraps make great compost. (Just don't put in any meat scraps or coffee grounds!)

Every few days, use a small rake to mix up your compost, then moisten it with a plant mister. Doing these things will help nature recycle your garbage faster. You can also keep adding more grass clippings and leaves. It will take one to four months to turn your garbage into fertilizer, depending on variables such as the temperature and humidity. Then you can use the fertilizer to help plants grow in a garden.

Bottle Terrarium

Recycle old pop bottles by turning them into habitats for houseplants.

What You'll Need:

2-liter soda bottle with black plastic base

scissors

plants

potting soil

charcoal for houseplants

FIRST REMOVE THE BLACK PLASTIC BASE from the bottom of your soda bottle and set it aside. This will be the bottom of your terrarium.

Use scissors to cut off the top of the bottle just below the "shoulder" of the bottle. When turned over, the bottle forms a clear dome over your terrarium.

Now sprinkle about ½ inch of crushed charcoal in the bottom of the black plastic base. Fill the base with potting soil up to about ½ inch from the top. Plant some small houseplants, woodland plants, seeds, or cuttings in the base. Water them until the soil is moist but not soggy. Cover the plants with the clear plastic dome you made from the rest of the bottle. Place your bottle terrarium in a sunny spot and water it regularly.

If you collect wild plants or seeds for your terrarium, always be sure to get permission before collecting on private property. Never collect plants from parks, state lands, or federal lands.

Speak Your Mind

Voice your opinion about something in nature that you really care about.

What You'll Need:

stationery

pen

stamp

envelope

ARE YOU CONCERNED about stray animals? Air pollution? The destruction of the rain forest? No matter where you live, you have people who represent you in government. Each area of the United States has two senators and at least one congressional representative. The job of these people is to listen to the people in their area and try to do something about their problems and concerns. So, why not write them a letter and tell them what's on your mind!

Be as specific as you can about what's bothering you. Tell them what you're doing to help and what you'd like them to do. Maybe they could try to get new laws passed to take better care of nature. You can even write to the president of the United States! After all, the president is your leader, too.

Another way to make your voice heard is to write a letter to the editor of your local newspaper. Every newspaper has a page where it prints letters from readers. Many people read these letters, so it's a chance to tell a lot of people how you feel. Here are the addresses of your government officials:

(Your U.S. senator's name)
U.S. Senate
Washington, DC 20510

(Your U.S. representative's name)
U.S. House of Representatives
Washington, DC 20515

(president's name)
The White House
1600 Pennsylvania Avenue
Washington, DC 20500

Index